SCIENCE FICTION AT LARGE

CONTRIBUTORS

Ursula K. Le Guin
Edward de Bono
John Taylor
John Brunner
Harry Harrison
Alvin Toffler
Alan Garner
Thomas M. Disch
Peter Nicholls
Robert Sheckley
Philip K. Dick

SCIENCE FICTION
AT LARGE

A collection of essays, by various
hands, about the interface between
science fiction and reality

Edited by

PETER NICHOLLS

HARPER & ROW, PUBLISHERS

New York, Hagerstown, San Francisco, London

FIRST U.S. EDITION

ISBN: 0-06-013198-5

LIBRARY OF CONGRESS CATALOG CARD NUMBER: 76-50161

77 78 79 80 81 10 9 8 7 6 5 4 3 2 1

CONTENTS

INTRODUCTION

PETER NICHOLLS

This book results from a series of lectures delivered at the Institute of Contemporary Arts in London, from January to March 1975. The lectures were part of an elaborate festival of science fiction which also involved a film/discussion series, a drama series for children, an art display, and even a section devoted to futuristic fashion design.

The over-all festival organiser was a young anthropologist called Ted Polhemus. He and I got together very early to discuss the shape of it, and I was given the responsibility of organising the lectures, and editing the resulting book. I did all this in my capacity as administrator of the Science Fiction Foundation at North East London Polytechnic, which sponsored the lecture series. (The Science Fiction Foundation is a small unit in the Faculty of Arts, devoted to co-ordinating research into science fiction in the UK, and to investigating the educational areas in which science fiction might usefully be put to work, both at school and university level.)

The lectures are printed in this book in exactly the order in which they were given, together with one extra contribution which could not be given as an actual lecture—the contribution from Philip K. Dick, who was prevented by ill-health from travelling to England and delivering it.

The pieces were all written for verbal delivery, and have both the strengths and the weaknesses this suggests. (One possible weakness, which I prefer to consider a strength, is the temptation, succumbed to by several of the speakers, to put their points in the most controversial possible manner, in order to evoke a direct response from the listeners, and bring about a lively question-and-answer period afterwards.)

There was a theory behind the lecture series. Basically, it is easiest to describe in negatives. We did not want to preach to the converted. We hoped, rather, to reach the silent majority, the general science fiction readership who, rightly or wrongly, would rather die than attend a science fiction convention, even supposing they were aware that such apparently grotesque phenomena actually exist in what they might fondly suppose to be a sane and ordered society.

Because the lecture series was to be delivered at the Institute of Contemporary Arts, I emphasised from the beginning that the speakers I wanted were all to be contemporary. If we did not invite Arthur Clarke or Robert Heinlein, it is because they are major figures who began their work a long time ago. But I saw the series in terms of a surf-board metaphor (my Australian blood speaking nostalgically to me). To ride the wave successfully, the board-rider must balance at the very curl, the downthrust of the breaking crest. I invited speakers (by no means all of the same age) who could fairly be seen as working in the areas where the wave is breaking (not always the same wave, either, but that's another question, taken up in one or two of the later chapters).

The next negative requirement was, that we did *not* want this to be a series about science fiction *per se*. The importance of science fiction can only be that it speaks to us of the real world. If, as some adverse critics claim, it is purely a literature of escapism, then there is no point in a lecture series in the first place. It followed then that the lectures should be located in the interface area—the area where science fiction meets real life. This is a bigger and more complex area than might be supposed, and its geography is sometimes obscure. The relationship of science fiction to the real world need not be literal. The science fiction which deliberately sets out to predict the nature of the future, for example, is only a tiny fraction of the whole. Science fiction works primarily through metaphor. To read it literally is not to hear its profoundest and most disturbing reverberations. Alan Garner, Ursula Le Guin, Tom Disch and Philip Dick, all in different ways, have observations to make in this area.

Each of the lectures, then, was to have a conjunction, to be 'science fiction *and*'. The implicit 'and' is usually clear enough. Edward de Bono, for example, speaks of science fiction and models of thought. Harry Harrison speaks of science fiction and history. Ursula Le Guin speaks of science fiction and human character. John Taylor speaks of science fiction and science. John Brunner speaks of science fiction and pseudo-science.

So we have, not science fiction behind closed walls, but 'science fiction at large'—out in the world where it is subjected, perhaps, to more searching scrutiny than it is often accorded by its more fanatical adherents, but also in a world which it speaks of and to, a world which ultimately, and in oblique ways, it probably affects radically. The signs and portents by which we live, the great images which we all share, even our aspirations, are constantly evolving. A semiologist might well, to take a simple example, be able to trace a revolution in popular feeling simply by studying the place of the rocket ship in popular symbology between 1930 and now. The primal images of science fiction are part, now, of the consciousness of people everywhere in a way that would have seemed impossible 40 years ago. This is an area of study where very little precise work has been done. It's sufficient at this point to suggest that, while science fiction may have little direct effect (I know of no established instances where cabinet meetings have been directly influenced by a science fiction book, though some cases have been rumoured), its indirect effect on the nature of our culture and our expectations must surely be strong indeed—even on people who have never consciously read any science fiction. The images of science fiction are not restricted to the cinema screen or the pages of books; they have insinuated themselves, by a process of osmosis, into the very style and air of our lives. Hence, as I say, our title: Science Fiction At Large.

The lecture series held many surprises. If it had been held only ten years ago, I have little doubt that every speaker would have seen his main duty to be missionary work—the earnest effort to convince a possibly doubting populace that science fiction deserves the right to be taken seriously. (There would be the usual embarrassed references to monster movies and whatever ur-*Star Trek* was popular then, together with the solemn injunction not to judge SF by its most infantile examples.)

None of this happened. Every speaker imagined it to be the most natural thing in the world that an audience should have spent hundreds of pounds in order to take part in a public discussion about science fiction. The end result of this access of self-confidence may strike some readers as paradoxical.

Generally (though not in every case) the speakers devoted a considerable amount of time and energy to saying what was *wrong* with science fiction. To my knowledge, this book constitutes an indictment of the genre more sweeping, though by no means total, than any that has ever appeared before, and very much better informed.

The point is this: the time of promoting science fiction as respectable in the eyes of the various literary and educational establishments is now passing. The next phase (a much more interesting one) is just opening up. This is the stage of discrimination, the sorting of wheat from chaff, the realisation that science fiction is not monolithic but, as Thomas M. Disch says later on, stratified into many different classes, each with a different social function, each with a different degree of sophistication and intent. The question is not, for example, should we use science fiction at schools? The question is, *what* science fiction should we use in schools, and what do we intend to do with it?

Also, we are reaching the phase of seeing science fiction as a cultural phenomenon, one that has lasted a long enough time for us to have a pretty good idea of its nature. Here, bad science fiction comes into its own. The implicit prejudices to be found in science fiction at its pulpiest level tell us much about the societies that have produced it. A literature with the staying power that science fiction has shown itself to possess, it cannot be stressed too strongly, is not only a fit subject for study, it is an essential subject for study. Science fiction is a measure of the times. In its complete bulk, it is a far more significant artefact than, say, the Empire State Building or any work more obviously built by the hand of man. (I would argue, given the time, that it is also a more significant artefact than the western, the thriller, the detective story and the popular romance— than any other of the popular genres of our society.)

Seven of the eleven pieces in the book are by science fiction writers, and the others are by workers in fields which are closely related, in one sense or another, to the areas which science fiction itself investigates; de Bono the psychologist, Taylor the scientist, Toffler the futurologist, and myself the critic. The articles by the science fiction writers will be of special interest to some readers for the double light they shed: an outward beam, which illuminates the science fiction field as a whole, and an inward beam, which lights up their own fiction. Some of the lectures were more objective than others, but I believe the 'double beam effect' works even in the cases of the two most personal contributions, those by Alan Garner and Philip K. Dick. It might even be said that these two extremely self-revelatory articles are the ones that, by implication, have the most to say about the creative process as a whole.

I do think that a rough consensus does emerge from the lectures about what science fiction is, and what it does, and what it should do. The consensus may not be assented to by the reader, of course. The controversial aspects of this book are what, I believe, make it such a peculiarly useful introduction to the genre itself.

Here is science fiction, released from its cage, prowling the world at large.

Science Fiction and Mrs Brown

URSULA K. LE GUIN

URSULA K. LE GUIN

Ursula Le Guin has risen very quickly; in less than a decade she has reached a secure position in the science fiction pantheon. She has won many awards, both Hugos and Nebulas. Her best known work includes the "Earthsea" trilogy for children, *The Left Hand of Darkness*, *The Lathe of Heaven* and *The Dispossessed*.

When I went to Heathrow Airport to meet her, I only had a photograph printed on the back of a book jacket to use as identification. When she walked past, I missed her completely. She was very much *smaller* than I had expected. She spoke very quietly. Would she be able to project her voice, her personality, across a large lecture theatre, I wondered (after I found her, fifteen minutes later). I needn't have worried.

Ursula is by no means as vulnerable as she looks. Standing perfectly still at the lectern, even though she was reading her prepared script word for word, she nevertheless seemed to speak directly to the audience as individuals. She was greeted by an absorbed and total silence while she spoke, and by a standing ovation when she had finished. It was not until then that I realised just how many people shared my enthusiasm for her, how important she has become in science fiction. That night in London she was a super-star. The series could not have got off to a better start, a start which so ringingly affirmed the humanity without which the science fiction that matters most cannot flourish.

'She looked very small, very tenacious; at once very frail and very heroic. And I have never seen her again.'

This Mrs Brown, says Virginia Woolf, is the subject matter of the novel. She appears to the novelist, inside a railway carriage or inside the mind, and she says, Catch me if you can!

> I believe that all novels begin with an old lady in the corner opposite. I believe that all novels, that is to say, deal with character, and that it is to express character—not to preach doctrines, sing songs, or celebrate the glories of the British Empire, that the form of the novel, so clumsy, verbose, and undramatic, so rich, elastic, and alive, has been evolved. . . . The great novelists have brought us to see whatever they wish us to see through some character. Otherwise they would not be novelists, but poets, historians, or pamphleteers. (*ibid.*)

I accept this definition. I don't know if it is a critically fashionable one at the moment, and really don't care; it may seem banal to critics who love to talk about epiphanies, apocalypses, and other dim religious polysyllables, but to a novelist—this novelist, at any rate—it is simply, and profoundly, and in one syllable, true.

It was true in 1865, when Mrs Brown was named Sarah Gamp; it was true in 1925, when Mrs Brown was named Leopold Bloom; it is true in 1975. Mrs Brown's name in England today is Rose, in Margaret Drabble's *The Needle's Eye*; Silvia, in Angus Wilson's *Late Call*. She is Leni, in Heinrich Böll's *Group Portrait with Lady*. She has found her way to Australia, where her name is Voss, or Laura. She has never left Russia, where her name is of course Natasha or Anna or Raskolnikov, but also Yury Zhivago, and Ivan Denisovitch. Mrs Brown turns up in India, in Africa, in South America, wherever novels are written. For as Mrs Woolf said, 'Mrs Brown is eternal. Mrs Brown is human nature. Mrs Brown changes only on the surface; it is the novelists who get in and out. There she sits. . . .'

There she sits. And what I am curious about is this: Can the writer of science fiction sit down across from her? Is it possible? Have we any hope of catching Mrs Brown, or are we trapped for good inside our great, gleaming spaceships hurtling out across the galaxy, antiseptic vehicles moving faster than the

Just about 50 years ago, a woman named Virginia Woolf sat down in a carriage in the train going from Richmond to Waterloo, across from another woman, whose name we don't know. Mrs Woolf didn't know it either; she called her Mrs Brown.

> She was one of those clean, threadbare old ladies whose extreme tidiness—everything buttoned, fastened, tied together, mended, and brushed up—suggests more extreme poverty than rags and dirt. There was something pinched about her—a look of suffering, of apprehension, and, in addition, she was extremely small. Her feet, in their clean little boots, scarcely touched the floor. I felt that she had nobody to support her; that she had to make up her mind for herself; that, having been deserted, or left a widow, years ago, she had led an anxious, harried life, bringing up an only son, perhaps, who, as likely as not, was by this time beginning to go to the bad. ("Mr Bennett and Mrs Brown")

Mrs Woolf, who was an inveterate snooper, listened to the fragmentary conversation between the old lady and the man travelling with her—dull comments, snatches of incomprehensible business. Then all of a sudden Mrs Brown said, 'Can you tell me if an oak trees dies when the leaves have been eaten for two years in succession by caterpillars?' She spoke quite brightly, and rather precisely, in a cultivated, inquisitive voice. And while her companion was replying at length about plagues of insects at his brother's farm in Kent, Mrs Brown took out a little white handkerchief and began to cry, very quietly, which annoyed the man. And then he got off at Clapham Junction; and then she got off at Waterloo. 'I watched her disappear, carrying her bag, into the vast blazing station,' says Mrs Woolf.

Richmond–Waterloo train, faster than the speed of light, ships capable of containing heroic captains in black and silver uniforms, and second officers with peculiar ears, and mad scientists with nubile daughters, ships capable of blasting other, inimical ships into smithereens with their apocalyptic, holocaustic rayguns, and of bringing loads of colonists from Earth to unknown worlds inhabited by incredibly sinister or beautiful forms of alien life, ships capable of anything, absolutely anything, except one thing: they cannot contain Mrs Brown. She simply doesn't fit. It's funny, the idea of Mrs Brown in a spaceship. She's much too small to visit a Galactic empire or to orbit a neutron star. 'Her feet, in their clean little boots, scarcely touched the floor.' Or is that quite it? Could it be that Mrs Brown is actually, in some way, too large for the spaceship? That she is, you might say, too *round* for it—so that when she steps into it, somehow it all shrinks to a shiny tin gadget, and the heroic captains turn to cardboard, and the sinister and beautiful aliens suddenly appear to be, most strangely, not alien at all, but mere elements of Mrs Brown herself, lifelong and familiar, though startling, inhabitants of Mrs Brown's unconscious mind?

So that's my first question: Can Mrs Brown and science fiction ever sit down together in the same railway carriage, or space ship? Or to put it plainly, Can a science fiction writer write a novel?

And then there will be a second question: Is it advisable, is it desirable, that this should come to pass? But I will come back to that later on.

I suspect that Virginia Woolf would have answered my first question with a characteristically subtle and apparently tentative but quietly decisive No. But in 1923 when she wrote the essay "Mr Bennett and Mrs Brown" she really could not have answered it, for there was very little science fiction available to her eye and judgement. H. G. Wells's scientific romances were a quarter-century old; he had put them behind him and was busy writing Utopias—Utopias of which Virginia Woolf said, very decisively indeed, 'There are no Mrs Browns in Utopia'. And she was absolutely right.

But even as she said it, a book was being published in England, and another was being written in America; very strange books, written under strange circumstances, which prevented their receiving much critical notice or general attention. The one printed in England was written by a Russian, Zamyatin, in Russian, though it was not, and has never been, published in Russia. It has existed for 50 years only in foreign editions and in translation—in exile. Its author died in exile. The pattern is not wholly unfamiliar, now. As for the other book, it was not written for publication at all, and was published only after the death of the author, Austin Tappan Wright, in 1942.

A quite good simple test to detect the presence or absence of Mrs Brown in a work of fiction is this: A month or so after reading the book, can you remember her name? It's silly, but it works pretty well. For instance, almost anybody who reads *Pride and Prejudice* will remember the names Elizabeth and Darcy, probably for very much longer than a month. But anyone who has read one of Mr Norman Mailer's works of fiction need not apologise if he can't remember a single name from it—except one, of course: that of Norman Mailer. Because Mr Mailer's books aren't about Mrs Brown, they're about Mr Mailer. He is a marvellous writer, but not a novelist. Very few Americans are. You see, it does work, roughly. But the first use I want to make of it on science fiction is an acid test, and I admit I failed it. I could remember only two of the three main characters' names. The women are 0, and I–330; and there's that wonderful minor character named S; but what's the name of the narrator, the central character? Oh, damn. I had to look at my copy of the book. D–503, of course, that's it. That's him. I will never forget him, poor soul; but I did forget his number. I plead the fact that I sometimes forget the telephone number we have had for sixteen years. I am very poor at mathematics. But I have sat facing D–503, not in a railway carriage to be sure, but in a great glass-walled, glass-floored, glass-roofed, super-Utopian building; have suffered with him; escaped with him; been recaptured, and dragged back to Utopia, and lobotomised, with him; and I will not forget it. Nor the book's name, *We*, nor its author's name, Yevgeny Zamyatin, the author of the first science fiction novel.

We is a dystopia which contains a hidden or implied Utopia; a subtle, brilliant, and powerful book; emotionally stunning, and technically, in its use of the metaphorical range of science fiction, still far in advance of most books written since. Austin Tappan Wright's novel *Islandia* is quite another kettle of fish. It is old-fashioned. It does not look forward; neither does it look back. It looks sideways. It does not offer a Utopia, but merely an alternative. And the alternative seems, on the surface of it, an escapist one, a mere daydream. A life-long daydream. A book written by a successful lawyer, secretly, for his private solace and delight; a child's imaginary country, maps and all, carried on for 30 years, a huge manuscript, whole volumes on the geology of the continent of Islandia, its history, its institutions. . . . And also a story. A narrative, with characters. The author's daughter extracted the story, Knopf published it, and a few people found it. And since then there have always been a few people who find it, and who treasure it. It is not a great book perhaps, but a singularly durable one, and a durably singular one. There is nothing else in all literature like *Islandia*. It is a life work; Wright put himself into it totally. It is a genuinely alternative society, worked out thoroughly, pragmatically, and humanely. And it is a novel. It is full of real people. There is plenty of room in Islandia for Mrs Brown. That, in fact, is the point of it. I think that Wright saw a world, his America, his century, becoming psychotic, depersonalised, unliveable, and so he created a non-existent continent, geology and weather and rivers and cities and houses and weaving-looms and fireplaces and politicians and farmers and house-wives and manners and misunderstandings and love-affairs and all, for human beings to inhabit. And thus he rendered questionable Virginia Woolf's statement, 'There are no Mrs Browns in Utopia'. I think it possible she might have been quite pleased to know it.

But meanwhile, while Austin Tappan Wright is scribbling happily in his study, and Zamyatin is silent in exile in Paris, the 1930s are upon us, and science fiction is getting underway. The first rockets leave the launching pad. Decades of thrilling adventures ensue. Evil Venusians are thwarted. Scientists' nubile daughters are rescued, squeaking. Galactic empires rise and fall. Planets are bought and sold. Robots receive the Tablets of the Three Laws from Mount Sinai. Marvellous hardware is invented. Humanity grows old, destroys itself, redeems itself, replaces itself, transcends itself, reverts to bestiality, becomes God. The stars go out. The stars blink on again, like neon signs. Awful and wonderful tales are told—truly wonderful, some of them; some of them really awful. But in none of the spaceships, on none of the planets, in none of the delightful, frightening, imaginative, crazy, clever stories are there any people. There is Humanity, and After, as in Stapledon. There is Inhumanity, and After, as in Orwell and Huxley. There are captains and troopers, and aliens and maidens and scientists, and emperors and robots and monsters—all signs, all symbols, statements, effigies, allegories, everything between the Stereotype and the Archetype. But not Mrs Brown. Name me a name. There are no names. The names don't matter. The names are mere labels—Gagarin, Glenn—symbols, heroic labels, names of astronauts. The humanity of the astronaut is a liability, a weakness, irrelevant to his mission. As astronaut, he is not a being: he is an act. It is the act that counts. We are in the age of Science, where nothing *is*. None of the scientists, none of the philosophers, can say what anything or anyone is. They can only say, accurately, beautifully, what it does. The age of Technology; of Behaviourism; the age of the Act.

And then?

Well, then, as the century nears its midpoint and the Act seems to be heading ever more inevitably towards a tragic dénouement, there comes along the most improbable Mrs Brown we have yet seen, and coming from the most improbable direction. It must be some kind of sign and portent. If any field of literature has no, can have no Mrs Browns in it, it is fantasy—straight fantasy, the modern descendant of folktale, fairytale, and myth. These genres deal with archetypes, not with characters. The very essence of Elfland is that Mrs Brown can't get there—not unless she is changed, changed utterly, into an old mad witch, or a fair young princess, or a loathely Worm.

But who is this character, then, who really looks very like Mrs Brown, except that he has furry feet; a short, thin, tired-looking fellow, wearing a gold ring on a chain round his neck, and heading rather disconsolately eastward, on foot? I think you know his name.

Actually, I will not argue hard in defence of Frodo Baggins as a genuine, fully-developed, novelistic character; as I say, his importance to my theme here is rather as a sign and portent. If you put Frodo together into one piece with Sam, and with Gollum, and with Sméagol—and they fit together into one piece—you get, indeed, a complex and fascinating character. But, as traditional myths and folktales break the complex conscious daylight personality down into its archetypal unconscious dreamtime components, Mrs Brown becoming a princess, a toad, a worm, a witch, a child—so Tolkien in his wisdom broke Frodo into four: Frodo, Sam, Sméagol, and Gollum; perhaps five, counting Bilbo. Gollum is probably the best character in the book because he got two of the components, Sméagol and Gollum, or as Sam calls them, Slinker and Stinker. Frodo himself is only a quarter or a fifth of himself. Yet even so he is something new to fantasy: a vulnerable, limited, rather unpredictable hero, who finally fails at his own quest—fails it at the very end of it, and has to have it accomplished for him by his mortal enemy, Gollum, who is, however, his kinsman, his brother, in fact himself. . . . And who then goes home to the Shire, very much as Mrs Brown would do if she only had the chance; but then he has to go on, leave home, make the voyage out, in fact die—something fantasy heroes never do, and allegories are incapable of doing.

I shall never cease to wonder at the critics who find Tolkien a 'simple' writer. What marvellously simple minds they must have!

So now we have got a kind of primitive version of Mrs Brown into fantasy, the ancient kingdom of which science fiction is a modern province. There she stands, quite steady on her furry feet. And we have met her twice in the borderlands of Utopia. But there haven't been any Utopias written for decades; the genre seems to have turned inside out, becoming purely satirical and admonitory. And what about science fiction proper? As we come into the '60s and '70s, and a new kind of writer is writing science fiction, and science fiction is even being printed on a new kind of paper which doesn't get yellow and crumbly at the edges quite so fast, and as the real rockets really take off and land on the real Moon and thus leave science fiction free to stop describing the future and to start imagining it—do we, now, find any more room in the spaceship for **Mrs Brown?**

I am not sure.

I am going to have to talk about myself and my own work for a while here; but before I do so—and so that I don't seem to be setting myself up as a kind of stout Cortez, silent upon a peak in Disneyland, sole discoverer of uncharted seas—let me mention a couple of names.

Mrs Thea Cadence.

Mr Nobusuke Tagomi.

Do those names mean anything to you? They do to me; a good deal. They are the names of two of the first Mrs Browns I met in modern science fiction.

Mr Tagomi turns up in Philip K. Dick's *Man in the High Castle*. Thea is the protagonist of D. G. Compton's *Synthajoy*.

They are not unique; they're rare birds, still, in science fiction, but not unique. I just picked those two because I like them. I like them as people. They are people. Characters. Round, solid, knobby. Human beings, with angles and protuberances to them, hard parts and soft parts, depths and heights.

They also stand for a great deal, of course. They are exemplars, teaching aids if you like; they express something the authors wanted urgently to say as clearly as possible. Something about human beings under stress, under peculiarly modern forms of moral pressure.

If the authors wanted to speak clearly why didn't they write an essay, a documentary, a philosophical or sociological or psychological study?

Because they are both novelists. Real novelists. They write science fiction, I imagine, because what they have to say is best said using the tools of science fiction, and the craftsman knows his tools. And still, they are novelists, because while using the great range of imagery available to science fiction, they say what it is they have to say through a character—not a mouthpiece, but a fully realised secondary creation. The character is primary. And what used to be the entire object of science fiction—the invention of miraculous gadgets, the relation of alternate histories, and so on—is now used subjectively, as a metaphor, as a means for exploring and explaining what goes on inside Mrs Brown, or Thea, or Tagomi. The writers' interest is no longer really in the gadget, or the size of the universe, or the laws of robotics, or the destiny of social classes, or anything describable in quantitative, or mechanical, or objective terms. They are not interested in what things do, but in how things are. Their subject is the subject, that which cannot be other than subject: ourselves. Human beings.

But these are human beings who live in the universe as seen by modern science, and in the world as transformed by modern technology. That is where science fiction still remains distinct from the rest of fiction. The presence of science and technology is essential, in both these books. It is the given. Only, as I say, the speculations and facts, the idea of relativity, the idea of a machine to reproduce emotions, are not used as ends in themselves, but as metaphors. Metaphors for what? For what is not given; an x; an x which the writers are pursuing. The elusive individual, upon whom all the givens act, but who simply is. The person, the human psyche, life, Mrs Brown, 'the spirit we live by'. Catch me if you can! And I think they caught her. She's there. Thea, shrewd and tragic in her madhouse, Mr Tagomi, shrewd and tragic in his business office, both of them trying, in a half-conscious, muddled agony, to reach freedom, both failing or succeeding depending on how you look at it, 'very small, and very tenacious, at once very frail and very heroic. . . .'

Welcome aboard the space ship, Mrs Brown.

Angus Wilson (whose book *The Old Men at the Zoo* is quite definable as science fiction, by the way, although I doubt he'd much like to have it *categorised* as science fiction) has described, in *The Wild Garden*, the way a novel first came to him.

> In my original conception of *Hemlock and After* . . . I saw Mrs Curry, obese, sweet, and menacing, certain in her hysteric sense of power that she can destroy a good man, Bernard Sands; and because my vision is primarily ironic, I saw Bernard painfully thin, bitter, inward-turning . . . A momentary powerful visual picture of a fat woman and a thin man. The whole of the rest of the novel, for good or bad, is simply an extension needed, as I thought, to communicate this very visual ironic picture to others. . . .

The novels, in fact, *are* those moments of vision. No didactic, sociological, psychological, or technical elaboration can alter that significance for the novelist himself. Like any other artist's, the novelist's statement is a concentrated vision . . . but unlike the others he has chosen the most difficult of all forms, one that makes its own discipline as it goes along. We can never hope for perfection . . . that other arts can achieve. But any serious novelist who . . . does not announce this vision as his central impulse is either playing down to some imaginary 'plain chap' audience or has forgotten his original true inspiration in the polemics of moral, social, or formal purpose. Everyone says as a commonplace that a novel is an extended metaphor, but too few, perhaps, insist that the metaphor is everything, the extension only the means of expression.

That is splendid, and splendidly continues the Virginia Woolf quotations with which I started. It moves me very much, because it states my own experience very nearly. A book does not come to me as an idea, or a plot, or an event, or a society, or a message; it comes to me as a person. A person seen, seen at a certain distance, usually in a landscape. The place is there, the person is there. I didn't invent him, I didn't make her up: he or she is there. And my business is to get there too.

Once, like Mr Wilson, I saw two of them. As my vision is not ironic, but romantic, they were small figures, remote, in a tremendous waste landscape of ice and snow. They were pulling a sledge or something over the ice, hauling together. That is all I saw. I didn't know who they were. I didn't even know what sex they were (I must say I was surprised when I found out). But that is how my novel *The Left Hand of Darkness* began, and when I think of the book, it is still that vision I see. All the rest of it, with all its strange rearrangements of human gender and its imagery of betrayal, loneliness, and cold, is my effort to catch up, to get nearer, to get there, where I had seen those two figures on the snow, isolated and together.

The origin of my book *The Dispossessed* was equally clear, but it got very muddled before it ever came clear again. It too began with a person, seen much closer to, this time, and with intense vividness: a man, this time; a scientist, a physicist in

fact; I saw the face more clearly than usual, a thin face, large
clear eyes, and large ears—these, I think, may have come from
a childhood memory of Robert Oppenheimer as a young man.
But more vivid than any visual detail was the personality, which
was most attractive—attractive, I mean, as a flame to a moth.
There, there he is, I have got to get there this time. . .

My first effort to catch him was a short story. I should have
known he was much too big for a short story. It's a writer's
business to develop an infallible sense for the proper size and
length of a work; the beauty of the novella and novel is
essentially architectural, the beauty of proportion. It was a
really terrible story, one of the worst I have written in 30 years
of malpractice. This scientist was escaping from a sort of
prison-camp planet, a stellar Gulag, and he gets to the rich
comfortable spoiled sister planet, and finally can't stand it
despite a love-affair there, and so re-escapes and goes back to
the Gulag, sadly but nobly. Nobly but feeble-mindedly. Oh,
it was a stupid story. All the metaphors were mixed. I hadn't
got anywhere near him. I'd missed him by so far, in fact, that I
hadn't damaged him at all. There he stood, quite untouched.
Catch me if you can!

All right. All right, what's-your-name. What is your name,
by the way? Shevek, he told me promptly. All right, Shevek. So
who are you? His answer was less certain this time. I think, he
said, that I am a citizen of Utopia.

Very well. That sounded reasonable. There was something
so decent about him, he was so intelligent and yet so disarmingly
naïve, that he might well come from a better place than this. But
where? The better place; no place. What did I know about
Utopia? Scraps of More, fragments of Wells, Hudson, Morris.
Nothing. It took me years of reading and pondering and
muddling, and much assistance from Engels, Marx, Godwin,
Goldman, Goodman, and above all Shelley and Kropotkin,
before I could begin to see where he came from, and could see
the landscape about him—and yes, in a way it was a prison
camp, but what a difference!—and the other people, the people
whom his eyes saw; and the place, the other place, to which
he was going, and from which I now knew, as he had always
known, *why* he must return.

Thus in the process of trying to find out who and what Shevek was, I found out a great deal else, and thought as hard as I was capable of thinking, about society, about my world, and about myself. I would not have found out or been able to communicate any of this if I had not been doggedly pursuing, through all byways and side-roads, the elusive Mrs Brown.

The book that resulted is a Utopia, of sorts; it is didactic, therefore, satirical, and idealistic. It is a thematic novel, in Angus Wilson's definition, in that it does not entirely manage to 'disseminate the moral proposition so completely in a mass of living experience that it is never directly sensed as you read but only apprehended at the end as a result of the life you have shared in the book. This,' Mr Wilson goes on, 'is the real challenge and triumph of the novel.' (*The Wild Garden*) I did not fully meet that challenge or achieve that triumph. The moral proposition of *The Dispossessed* is sometimes fully embodied, sometimes not. The sound of axes being ground is occasionally audible. Yet I do believe that it is, basically, a novel, because at the heart of it you will not find an idea, or an inspirational message, or even a stone axe, but something much frailer and obscurer and more complex: a person. I have been strengthened in this belief by noticing that almost every reviewer, however carried away he gets in supporting or attacking or explaining the book's themes and ideas, somewhere in the discussion has mentioned its protagonist by name. There he is!—there, if only for a moment. If I had to invent two entire worlds to get to him, two worlds and all their woes, it was worth it. If I could give the readers one glimpse of what I saw: Shevek, Mrs Brown, the Other, a soul, a human soul, 'the spirit we live by . . . '

I suppose I have answered my second question before I got around to asking it. It was, if you remember, Should a book of science fiction be a novel? If it is possible, all the same is it advisable or desirable that the science fiction writer be also a novelist of character?

I have already said yes. I have already admitted that this, to me, is the whole point. That no other form of prose, to me, is a patch on the novel. That if we can't catch Mrs Brown, if only for a moment, then all the beautiful faster-than-light ships, all the irony and imagination and knowledge and invention are in vain; we might as well write tracts or comic-books, for we will never be real artists.

So then let me play my own enemy for a little, and try to argue the other side: the anti-novel, or post-novel, point of view, which says that science fictioneers will never be novelists, and a good thing too.

From this point of view, the novel, the novel of character, is dead—as dead as the heroic couplet, and for the same reason: the times have changed. Such writers as Wilson and Drabble are mere epigones, draining the last dregs of an emptied cask; such writers as Bhattacharya and García Márquez flourish only because their countries are marginal to the place of origin of the novel, which was late in arriving at the periphery and correspondingly late in dying there. The novel is dead; and the task, the hope, of a new form such as science fiction is not to continue the novel, or to revitalise it, but to replace it.

There is, really, no Mrs Brown any more. There are only classes, masses, statistics, body-counts, subscription-lists, insurance risks, consumers, randomly selected samples, and victims. Or, if somewhere beyond all the quantification some hint of quality remains, some wisp of Mrs Brown, she is not to be reached any longer with any of the traditional tools of fiction. No one can catch her. She has been too profoundly changed by our life, and too rapidly changed. Mrs Brown herself has attained the speed of light, and become invisible to our finest telescopes. What is 'human nature' now, who dares talk about it seriously, in 1975? Has it any recognisable relation to what was called 'human nature' in the novel a century ago, which we now see as one tiny, limited fragment of the vast range of human variety and potentiality? The subject matter of the novel was the conscious, articulate portion of the minds of certain Europeans and North Americans, mostly white, mostly Christian, mostly middle class, mostly quite unaffected by science and, though affected by technology, totally uninterested in it; a handful of natives intensely interesting to the ethnologist because of their elaborate developments of manners, and their extraordinary absorption in interpersonal relationships. They thought their nature was human nature; but we don't; we can't. They thought themselves a norm; we have no norm. Through technology, which lets us travel and converse, and through such sciences as anthropology and psychology, we have learned too much about the complexity and variety of human behaviour and the even vaster complexity of the human mind, conscious and unconscious; we have learned, that is, that we really know almost nothing at all. Nothing solid is left, nothing to take hold of.

For an example of solidity, look at Mrs Sarah Gamp. There she is. Everything about her is almost appallingly solid. She represents a definite, established social stratum, though I, an ignorant American, won't try to specify it exactly. She is English; she is white; she is Christian—at least, she would say she's Christian. She is a product of urbanisation and the Industrial Revolution, but her traditions are much older than that, and you would find her ancestors hanging harpy-like about the bedsides of Ovid and Orestes. She is fixed in history, and in custom, and in her own self-opinion. She knows who she is and she knows what she wants. What she wants is a bottle to be placed handy on the mantelpiece, to which she 'may place her lips from time to time when so dispoged'.

Now what is a modern, 1975 equivalent to Mrs Gamp? Let me, to avoid odious comparisons, simply invent one. She would be younger than Mrs Gamp, most likely. She might not bathe any oftener. If she was a Christian, she might be a Jesus freak, but more probably she would be on some kind of vague occultist trip, or into Astrology. She would probably be better clothed, fed, and housed than Mrs Gamp, and would take for granted some luxuries Mrs Gamp had never heard of—automobiles, bottled shampoo, television in the sickroom, penicillin, and so forth. She would, however, have very much less certainty as to her place in society; she might be quite unable to say either who she is or what she wants. She would almost certainly not have a bottle handy. She would have a needle handy. Her addiction would not be funny, as Mrs Gamp's, in its outrageous hypocrisy, is. It would be too visibly, drastically disastrous to be funny. She would be too far out of touch with daily reality, too incompetent, even to function as badly as Mrs Gamp does as a night nurse. And her involvement with criminality would be, like Mrs Gamp's, a desperate grasping at respectability, or at least at the hope of unlimited gin. Her involvement with the criminal and the violent would be passive, helpless, pointless. Indeed, wherever Mrs Gamp is most revoltingly indomitable, I see this modern version of her as most passive. It is very hard to loathe her, to laugh at her, or to love her—as we do Mrs Gamp; or at least Dickens did, and I do. She doesn't amount to enough. She is a drifter, a pawn, a fragment, jagged bits of a person never annealed, never grown to a whole. Is there enough of her, indeed, to enter a novel as a real character, enough to paint a portrait of? Isn't she, aren't we all, too battered, too changed and changeable, too whirled-about, future-shocked, relativised, and inconstant, ever to sit still for a painted portrait, ever to stay still long enough that the slow, clumsy art of the novelist can catch up with us?

Click, the camera-eye—a moment, not a person, not a portrait, only a single moment implying nothing before or after, no continuity, click. And the whirr of the movie camera, catching the moment as it dissolves into the next, unrelated moment. These are our arts. The technological arts, dependent upon an incredible refinement of machinery and a vast expense of mechanical energy, expression of a technological age. There is poetry, still, but there is no more Mrs Brown. There are snapshots of a woman at various moments. There are moving pictures of a woman in various places with various other persons. They do not add up to anything so solid, so fixed, so Victorian or medieval as a 'character' or even a personality. They are moments; moods; the poetry of flux; fragments of the fragmented, of the changing of the changed.

Do we not see this foreshadowed in the art of Virginia Woolf herself?

And what is science fiction at its best but just such a 'new tool' as Mrs Woolf avowedly sought for 50 years ago, a crazy, protean, left-handed monkey-wrench, which can be put to any use the craftsman has in mind—satire, extrapolation, prediction, absurdity, exactitude, exaggeration, warning, message-carrying, tale-telling, whatever you like—an infinitely expandable metaphor exactly suited to our expanding universe, a broken mirror, broken into numberless fragments, any one of which is capable of reflecting, for a moment, the left eye and the nose of the reader, and also the farthest stars shining in the depths of the remotest galaxy?

If science fiction is this, or is capable of being this, a true metaphor to our strange times, then surely it is rather stupid and reactionary to try to enclose it in the old limits of an old art—like trying to turn a nuclear reactor into a steam-engine. Why should anyone try to patch up this marvellously smashed mirror so that it can reflect poor old Mrs Brown—who may not even be amongst us any more? Do we care, in fact, if she's alive or dead?

Well, yes. Speaking strictly for myself—yes. I do care. If Mrs Brown is dead, you can take your galaxies and roll them up into a ball and throw them into the trashcan, for all I care. What good are all the objects in the universe, if there is no subject? It isn't that mankind is all that important. I don't think that Man is the measure of all things, or even of very many things. I don't think Man is the end or culmination of anything, and certainly not the centre of anything. What we are, who we are, and where we are going, I do not know, nor do I believe anybody who says he knows, except, possibly, Beethoven, in the last movement of the last symphony. All I know is that we are here, and that we are aware of the fact, and that it behoves us to be aware—to pay heed. For we are not objects. That is essential. We are subjects, and whoever amongst us treats us as objects is acting inhumanly, wrongly, against nature. And with us, nature, the great Object, its tirelessly burning suns, its turning galaxies and planets, its rocks, seas, fish and ferns and fir-trees and little furry animals, all have become, also, subjects. As we are part of them, so they are part of us. Bone of our bone, flesh of our flesh. We are their consciousness. If we stop looking, the world goes blind. If we cease to speak and listen, the world goes deaf and dumb. If we stop thinking, there is no thought. If we destroy ourselves, we destroy consciousness.

And all this, the seeing, hearing, speaking, thinking, feeling —all this we do one by one. The great mystics have gone deeper than community and sensed identity, the identity of all; but we ordinary souls cannot do that, or only for a moment, maybe one moment in a lifetime. One by one we live, soul by soul. The person, the single person. Community is the best we can hope for, and community for most people means *touch*: the touch of your hand against the other's hand, the job done together, the sledge hauled together, the dance danced together, the child conceived together. We have only one body apiece, and two hands. We can form a circle, but we cannot *be* a circle. The circle, the true society, is formed of single bodies and single souls. If not, it is not formed at all. Only a mechanical, insensate imitation of true society, true community, is made up out of objectified, quantified, persons—a social class, a nation-state, an army, a corporation, a power bloc. There is no more hope in that direction. We have followed it to the end. I really see no hope anywhere except in Mrs Brown.

Most of us these days could do with a little hope; and I incline to think that you as readers have a right to ask—not to demand, never to demand, but to ask—for some hope from our arts. We really cannot ask for it from science. Science isn't in the hope business, and never was. When it offers us something affirmative, it's a mere spin-off, a secondary application; meanwhile science proceeds on its true course, which is towards an ever closer imitation of nature, an ever completer objectivity. The freer science is to proceed thus towards the inevitable, the freer it leaves art in its own domain of subjectivity, where it can play, in its own way, and if it has the courage, with nature, and with science itself, our surrogate nature.

In Stanislaw Lem's *The Invincible*, the protagonist Rohan and others of the crew of the starship 'Invincible' face a hostile and enigmatic world. They gradually develop an elegant explanation of the nature of that world, a literally mechanical explanation; but the explanation isn't the point of the book. It's not a mystery story. The book's theme is moral, and its climax is an extremely difficult ethical choice made by an individual. Neither reward nor punishment ensues. All that we and Rohan have learned is something about himself, and something about what is, and what is not, invincible. In Lem's *Solaris*, the protagonist takes on a world which cannot be understood objectively at all. A large part of the book is Lem's delighted, Borgesian send-up of the efforts of scientists to explain the planet Solaris, which resists and confounds them all, and yet which participates in the very deepest psychic motivations and troubles of the protagonist Kelvin, so that in the end, if he has not understood Solaris, yet Solaris seems in a way to have understood him. The dazzlingly rich, inventive, and complex metaphors of these novels serve to express, or symbolise, or illuminate the mind and emotions of late-twentieth-century man as exactly and as powerfully as the slums of London, the Court of Chancery, the Circumlocution Office, and Mrs Gamp's bottle served Dickens to illuminate the characters and destinies of his contemporaries.

In the essay with which I began, Virginia Woolf was criticising the school of Arnold Bennett because, as she saw it, such writers had substituted the external, the objective—houses, occupations, rents, income, possessions, mannerisms, etc.—for the subject, in whom they were really no longer interested. They had deserted novel-writing for sociology. The modern 'psychological novel' is a similar case, usually being not a portrait of a person, but a case study. 'Socialist Realism' is another example of the same flight from subjectivity. And most science fiction has shown the same tendency. It may rise from a yearning for the seemingly godlike detachment of the scientist, but what it results in is an evasion of the artist's obligation to reproduce—indirectly, for it cannot be reproduced directly—a vision. Science fiction has mostly settled for a pseudo-objective listing of marvels and wonders and horrors which illuminate nothing beyond themselves and are without real moral resonance: daydreams, wishful thinking, and nightmares. The invention is superb, but self-enclosed and sterile. And the more eccentric and childish side of science fiction fandom, the defensive, fanatic in-groups, both feed upon and nourish this kind of triviality, which is harmless in itself, but which degrades taste, by keeping publishers' standards, and readers' and critics' expectations, very low. It's as if they wanted us all to play poker without betting. But the real game is played for real stakes. It's a pity that this trivial image is perpetuated, when the work of people from Zamyatin to Lem has shown that when science fiction uses its limitless range of symbol and metaphor novelistically, with the subject at the centre, it can show us who we are, and where we are, and what choices face us, with unsurpassed clarity, and with a great and troubling beauty.

The beauty of fiction is always troubling, I suppose. It cannot offer transcendence, the peace that passes understanding, as poetry and music can: nor can it offer pure tragedy. It's too muddled. Its essence is muddle. Yet the novel, fiction concerned with individuals, in its stubborn assertion of human personality and human morality, does seem even now to affirm the existence of hope. Despite the best efforts of talented anti-novelists, it continues to avoid the clean and gleaming sterility of despair. It is muddled, elastic, inventive, adaptable.

It needs to be adaptable. These are bad times, and what is art to do in a bad time? Art never fed anyone—often not even the artist. Half the world is hungry, and art feeds only the spirit, on an immaterial food. Words, words, words. I may well live to eat my words.

But till then, here is what I think: I think art remains centrally important in any age, the best or the worst, because it doesn't lie. The hope it offers is not a false hope. And I think the novel is an important art, because it talks about what we live by, other than bread. And I think science fiction is—well, no, not important, yet still worth talking about, because it is a promise of continued life for the imagination, a good tool, an enlargement of consciousness, a possible glimpse, against a vast dark background, of the very frail, very heroic figure of Mrs Brown.

2

Lateral Thinking and Science Fiction

EDWARD DE BONO

Edward de Bono is a young-looking 42-year old doctor of medicine, born in Malta, educated in Oxford, and once a faculty member at Harvard. His field is not science fiction; nor is it medicine alone, though he is still a practising doctor. He is best known as a psychologist who specialises in thinking. He has written a number of books on the subject. Some of them have unspectacular, academic titles like *The Mechanism of Mind* and *The Use of Lateral Thinking*. Others have such titles as *The Dog Exercising Machine*. The unorthodoxy this suggests is by no means eccentricity, though it may help to explain his enormous popularity. Dr de Bono's name comes up in an amazing variety of contexts, but most often of all in arguments about education. Dr de Bono has not yet managed to revolutionise education in the UK, but he has catalysed an enormous amount of useful thinking about it.

I invited him to speak, because it seems to me that the 'lateral thinking' he talks about in his books has a great deal in common with the procedures of science fiction. When I invited him, I had no idea at all whether he had actually read any science fiction, but yes, he had, and yes, he'd be quite happy to talk about it. His lecture came early in the series, because I wanted to establish from close to the outset that these lectures were not to be about science fiction *per se*. They were to be about 'science fiction *and*'. The conjunction implied by the 'and' was, I hoped, to be with some subject generally recognised to be important, but not necessarily recognised as having anything to do with science fiction. Ursula Le Guin linked science fiction with people. Edward de Bono, the following week, went on to link science fiction with thinking. The two most important parameters were set up.

De Bono's lecture proved enormously popular. The hall (I supposed) was half full of psychology fans who knew nothing of science fiction, and half full of science fiction fans who knew nothing about psychology. Fifty people, without the sharp reflexes peculiar to science fiction fans and psychology fans, arrived late, and were turned away because the house was full. De Bono speaks fast, wittily, scribbling constantly on an overhead projector screen, undeterred by the fact that his illustrations were totally devoid of artistic merit. They worked anyway. The question period (which revealed that three-quarters of the audience knew a great deal about science fiction *and* psychology) would have been tough indeed for an inexperienced speaker, but Dr de Bono fielded all the questions with the effortless charm of the born lecturer.

He spoke without notes. His article below puts succinctly and rather more formally, exactly the case that he argued in the lecture. (Nothing has been added, though the joke about 'What flies at 600 miles an hour and is full of cucumber?' has tactfully been omitted. Answer:—thus proving that children are born lateral thinkers—'a jumbo jet pilot's sandwich'.)

The following piece was originally written for *Le Scienze* (the Italian edition of *Scientific American*). It was also used as a summary of an address given to the Royal Institution in London. The piece condenses into written form the gist of the talk given as part of the symposium on science fiction. The talk itself was designed as a talk and not as a paper and hence contained much material and a style that would have been rambling and repetitive in print. After all talks are perceptually constructed whereas papers tend to be logically constructed. In my talk I made no attempt to discuss science fiction directly but was content to describe the process and basis for what I call lateral thinking. This is because the parallelism between lateral thinking and science fiction is quite explicit—once you have seen it. Rather than discuss that relationship in advance I would prefer the reader to read through the piece treating it on its own merits and not deliberately relating it to science fiction. Having done that he may care to compare his own comments with mine.

Thinking and sex are undoubtedly the two most important human activities. Sex can look after itself, but what about thinking? Until man acquired the technological ability to destroy himself through errors in his thinking it did not much matter if thinking was also left to look after itself. Today it matters rather more. The traditional approaches to thinking have been four. First, the classical approach of philosophy with its creation of concepts in order to play circular word-games in which one always came back to the assumptions that had been made in the beginning. Second, the invention of separate artificial methods of handling information as in mathematics. This has been an immensely effective approach, but unfortunately cannot be applied directly to all situations. Third, the natural evolution of language and thinking habits aided occasionally by empirical observations. Fourth, the direct study of thinking as the behaviour of the physical system that is the brain.

Quite clearly, the last approach would be the most effective because it is the approach which has been used by science with such great success. The approach is to examine a given system in great detail. The more detail one has the more is one able to predict and alter its behaviour. This approach has worked from atomic energy to medicine, from chemistry to space travel. How near are we to knowing enough about the detailed workings of the brain to be able to understand the system and so use it more effectively?

The first purpose of science is simply to keep going. That is, to develop the present state of knowledge into the next state of knowledge, and so on. Ideas suggest experiments which, in turn, suggest new ideas and so there is always something to be done.

The second purpose of science is to produce something useful to man. It is assumed that this second purpose is automatically fulfilled by the first—the direct pursuit of knowledge for its own sake. It is also assumed that somewhere along the line this accumulating knowledge can be put to use. This system is effective, but it has two disadvantages. The first is that the areas of possible exploration have been growing so fast that there is no longer the money to support all possible exploration; and the second is that one may have to wait too long for enough pure knowledge to accumulate for it to become directly useful. So one may have to start trying to generate usefulness directly and not just as a by-product of knowledge pursued for its own sake.

In order to understand a system, science constructs a model of the features and relationships involved in that system and then studies how the model works in order to predict or influence the system's behaviour. The usual method of model-building is to study all the details as accurately as possible and then to see how these details fit together to give the complete model. This is the jig-saw approach. You find the small pieces and you put them together and, eventually, you will have the whole.

There is, however, another type of model which is constructed in exactly the opposite manner. Instead of pursuing detail one tries to get rid of all detail. One tries to construct systems that will operate in the same manner no matter what form the fine detail takes. This is much more like a mathematical model which is concerned with relationships rather than detail. For instance, instead of examining each switch and bulb and piece of wire in order to build up a picture of the lighting system in a house, one can look at a model of the broad type of system and then examine the behaviour of this type of system without waiting for the details of each switch (since the function of the switch would remain the same no matter how it was actually built).

So, instead of finding more and more detail, one proceeds to broader and broader types of system which do not depend on detail. Clearly, the broadest possible type of system includes all other systems and so is useless, but anything below that has a definite usefulness if one learns how to extract it.

It will be a long time before science has worked out all the details of the brain in a jig-saw fashion. A detailed examination of the components will not, by itself, be very helpful any more than a detailed examination of a building stone will give a picture of the architecture of Venice. The organisation of the system is as important, or more important, than the actual components. Yet science is more geared to study components than organisation. Do we have to wait until the full detail is worked out before we can say anything useful about the working of the brain in such matters as thinking?

If we do not want to wait, the only alternative is to look at certain broad types of information systems and make these types so broad that they cover various alternative forms of the detail involved. Then, having established that the mind is more likely to belong to one broad type of system than another, one sees what can be usefully derived from this. The result may be a myth, but then science consists of proceeding from one myth to a better one.

At first sight a horse and a motor-cycle seem to be similar systems. Both are used to travel from place to place. You sit astride both of them and steer both of them by moving the front end from side to side, but you would not get very far by whipping a faulty motor-cycle or filling a tired horse up with petrol! To use either system effectively it is not necessary to go into such details as the endocrinology of a horse or the physical chemistry of petrol combustion. It is enough to establish the broad type of system involved and the general principles that arise from each type of system: a dead horse cannot be revived but a dead motor-cycle can; a horse has some internal guidance system but a motor-cycle does not; a motor-cycle can be locked in a shed alone for months but a horse cannot.

Can we look at the brain in the same way, and at least establish what broad class of information system it is likely to belong to, and then, from this broad type of system, derive some useful general principles?

The two basic classes of information system can be described by models—the towel model and the jelly model. In the towel model a towel is laid out flat on a table and a small bowl of ink is placed nearby. A spoonful of ink is taken from the bowl and poured on to the surface of the towel at a specified place. The ink represents the 'information input' which can be specified by reference to co-ordinates taken along the edge of the towel. The information input is recorded as an ink stain. A number of different inputs are made one after another so that the towel comes to bear a number of ink stains. The towel simply records what has happened to it, and since the ink is immediately absorbed by the towel there is, at the end, an accurate record of the inputs.

The towel system is the sort of accurate memory system which one uses in a computer. The incoming information is recorded without being altered in any way. A separate processor then uses this stored information according to its programmed instructions. It is the processor that changes the information around.

In the jelly model the towel is replaced by a large shallow dish of ordinary jelly or gelatine. This time the bowl of ink is heated. When a spoonful of hot ink is poured on to the jelly it melts the jelly's surface. However, as the ink cools, it stops melting the jelly. When the cooling ink and melted jelly are poured off a shallow depression is left which marks where the ink was placed, and this depression corresponds to the ink stain in the towel model, as a record of input.

If succeeding spoonfuls of ink are poured on to widely separated parts of the jelly surface the final result is very much like the towel model, but if the spoonfuls overlap then something quite different happens. Instead of staying exactly where it has been placed, the incoming ink flows into an already existing depression and tends to make it deeper. At the end, instead of having a number of separate depressions, one has a sort of continuous channel which is sculpted into the surface of the jelly, much as a river is sculpted into the landscape.

The difference between the two types of recording system is considerable. With the towel model the ink stays where it is placed, so that, at the end, there is a good record of what has happened.

In the jelly model, however, the ink flows along the channels already formed in the surface. Thus, if a new spoonful of ink is placed at point G shown in Fig. 1 it does not stay there but flows

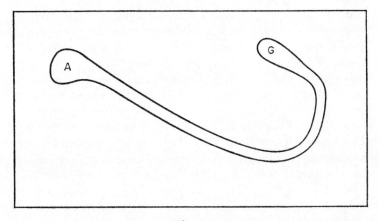

Fig. 1.

along the channel to end up at point A. Thus the G-information has been changed by the surface into A-information.

The jelly model is, therefore, a bad recording system since it does not record accurately but changes information around according to what has happened before. This is information-processing, and since the recording surface is now doing its own processing there is no need for an outside processor. Thus, the jelly model acts as an information processor or 'thinking system', although the surface is quite passive. All it does is to provide an opportunity for incoming information to organise itself into a pattern.

On different occasions I have asked some 5,000 scientists and mathematicians to give me a definition of pattern. Most of the definitions contain the necessary elements of order, recognition, repetition, and predictability. All these can be included under a very simple definition of a pattern: 'a pattern exists when the probability of one specified state succeeding another specified state is greater than chance.'

The degree of predictability indicates the strength of the pattern. Thus, the jelly model is really a pattern-making system since the ink flows in a predictable manner from one place to another with the surface organising incoming information into a pattern. In the towel model the incoming information is simply recorded and there is nothing to indicate which ink stain comes after which.

Instead of the jelly surface we can now consider a surface made up of a randomly-connected nerve network. Instead of ink flowing over the surface of the jelly we have an area of excitation flowing across the nerve network. Whether a particular nerve is excited or not depends on what happens at the synapse where it is affected by other nerves and different influences. If the sum total of the exciting influences, minus the inhibiting influences, is greater than the threshold the nerve fires but, if the threshold is not exceeded, the nerve remains silent. Thus, there are three variable factors: exciting influences, inhibiting influences, and any increase or fall in the threshold itself.

For the nerve network to function like the jelly model only two processes are required; firstly that an excited nerve should tend to excite those nerves connected to it, and secondly that excitation across a particular synapse in the past should lower the threshold to re-excitation of that synapse and that this effect should be cumulative. The above properties would be sufficient, but to make the system even more efficient at creating patterns from incoming information further features can be added: (a) a 'central inhibition' which is directly proportional to the total number of excited nerves and which feeds back to raise the threshold at all synapses. This ensures that a 'limited area' of excitation flows only over the most excitable nerves; (b) a 'tiring factor' so that, after a period of excitation, the threshold of a nerve rises and so it stops firing and becomes temporarily more resistant to further excitation. This ensures that an area of excitation will flow over the surface and not stay fixed in one place; (c) a 'rebound factor' so that, after the period of resistance mentioned above, the excited nerves again become more easy to excite than others. This is important for short-term memory and for the synthesis of information inputs.

All these factors and others are described in detail in my book *The Mechanism Of Mind* (published by Cape, 1969). There is no mystery about these properties. They are the known behaviour of nerves and nerve networks. All the evidence suggests that nerve networks act more like the jelly model than the towel model. Of course the jelly model is a very broad type of system. The important point is whether it is possible to derive anything

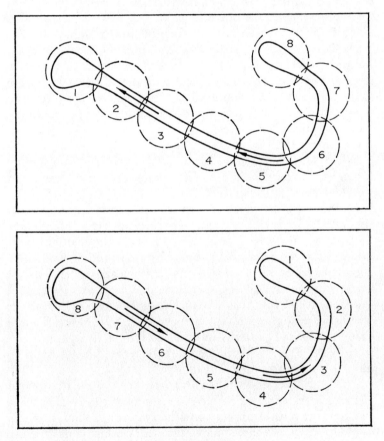

Fig. 2.

useful from a consideration of such a broad type of system, and in fact one can derive a number of important general principles from it. Two of these are described below. They arise directly from the nature of patterning systems.

In the towel model it does not matter at all in what sequence the ink stains are made since the result will be the same in the end. In the jelly model, however, the sequence is very important indeed. Fig. 2 shows what happens if the sequence is reversed —the channel flows on the opposite direction. Fig. 3 shows how there could be two separate channels flowing towards the centre if the sequence were different again. In any patterning system the sequence in which information is presented makes a huge difference to the outcome.

There is a very simple experiment which shows the importance of sequence in human thinking. Fig. 4 shows what happens when some plastic pieces are presented in a certain sequence to a person who is asked to arrange them at each stage to give a shape that would be easy to describe. The first two pieces are arranged to give a rectangle. The next piece is simply added to give a longer rectangle. However, with the next two pieces there is difficulty.

When, however, the plastic pieces are presented in a slightly different sequence there is no difficulty at all and the result is a simple square, as shown in Fig. 5.

In personal, cultural, social, or scientific experience information trickles in slowly over time and does not arrive all at once, and yet, at each stage, the best use has to be made of available information for one cannot wait for what comes next. The actual sequence in which the information arrives sets up the pattern or the way in which we look at a situation. Because of the sequence effect, these patterns do not necessarily make the best use of available information. One may have to break out of these established patterns in order to look at things in a different way. This is what is meant by the term, 'lateral thinking' and the process is part of creativity.

This is another effect that arises directly from the nature of a patterning system. In a patterning system one has no choice but to follow the most strongly-established pathway. Thus, in Fig. 6 one starts at B and moves along the wide pathway, missing the side turning. However, if somehow one could get to point S

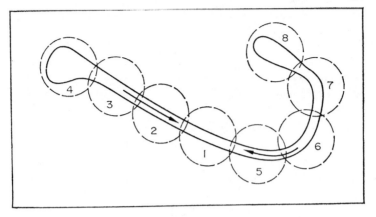

Fig. 3.

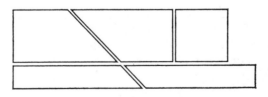

Fig. 4.

then, in hindsight, it is easy to see how one should have got there in the first place. This becomes obvious only after one has got there.

In an experiment I gave two small boards and a piece of string to one group of children. They were asked to use the boards to cross the floor of the room without touching the

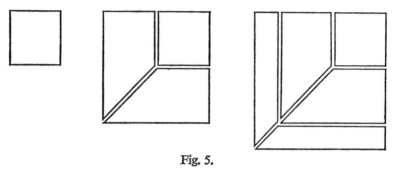

Fig. 5.

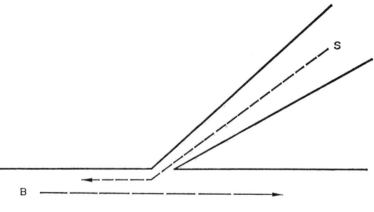

Fig. 6.

ground directly with their feet. They soon hit on the idea of standing on the first board and putting the second board in front of them. Then they stepped on the second board and picked up the first board to place in front of them again. In this way the boards were used as movable stepping stones. Some children tied the boards together with string so that they could pull on the string to retrieve the board that was behind them.

A second group of children was given the same problem but this time they only had one board each and the piece of string. After a while they found a completely different method. They tied the string to the front of the board and then, standing on the board, they hopped across the room at great speed, using the string to hold the board up against the soles of their feet. When the first group saw this method they all copied it because they found it so much better. Yet anyone in the two-board group could have used the one-board solution. This is so in theory, but in practice in a patterning system what is obvious in hindsight is not obvious in foresight.

In science, as in other areas, it is often the concepts we have that hold up progress more than the ones we do not have. Available and adequate ideas make it very difficult to come up with better ideas. For instance, the concept of guilt makes social misbehaviour more difficult to handle. Similarly, in psychology the concept of recall automatically shuts out whole types of memory system.

The major tool of Western culture thinking is the rejection principle crystallised in the word 'NO'. This is our basic selection tool since, by rejecting all arrangements of ideas that do not match with experience, we select what is left. 'NO' is a pattern-preserving device. The function of logical thinking is to extend or refine existing patterns but not to cut across them in order to put information together in a new way. However, as we have seen, in a patterning system the patterns set up by experience are not the only way of arranging available information or even the best way.

Humour and insight are the two phenomena of mind that illustrate the escape from the established way of looking at things. In humour one escapes from the existing pattern to find a new way of looking at things. This new way, however, is only just possible and is less plausible than the standard way. For example, the wife's reply to her husband who complains that the two clocks in the living room show different times: 'What would be the use of having two clocks in order to show one time?'

With insight, the escape is from a standard way of looking at things to a new way which is seen to be better as soon as it has been found. In trying to work out how many matches would be needed in a singles tennis tournament for which there were 111 entrants, for example, one could make a chart showing each match. However, if, instead of trying to find the winner, one tries to find the 110 losers then, since each player can only lose once and each game must have one loser, the answer is 110 matches.

However, both humour and insight are chance processes which occur haphazardly. This is because we have never developed any thinking tools for breaking out of patterns. On the contrary, all our thinking tools are designed to preserve patterns. We need a de-patterning device which can perform the same function in thinking that the de-patterning device of random mutation does in evolution. My suggestion is for a new word 'PO', which can be used as a tool for upsetting established patterns.

The first use of PO is to allow one to use ideas which do not match experience and which would therefore be rejected. With PO, instead of rejecting such ideas one uses them as stepping stones to go on to other ideas. Thus, PO allows one to use 'intermediate impossibles'. Because these 'impossible' ideas do not fit established patterns they allow one to step outside existing experience. The impossible idea is, however, only an intermediate stage on the way to reaching an idea which does make sense. As we have seen in a patterning system, once you have reached a new idea it is often possible in hindsight to see how that idea could have been reached in a logical fashion. This effect is shown in Fig. 7 where one has to pass through an

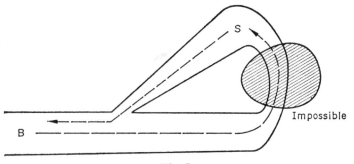

Fig. 7.

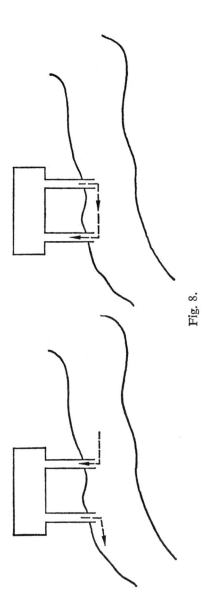

Fig. 8.

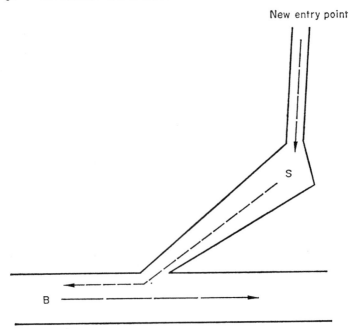

New entry point

S

B

Fig. 9.

impossible area in order to reach an idea which makes good sense. For example, in America, downstream pollution from factories sited along rivers is a big problem. The intermediate impossible is that factories should be placed downstream of themselves. This is obviously an impossible idea because the factory cannot be in two places at once, and yet, from it, one goes directly to the very reasonable idea of simply swopping over the inlet and outlet pipe so that the factory does, in fact, become 'downstream' of itself (Fig. 8).

When we look at any problem or situation we can only look at those things which experience has established as being part of the situation. Therefore, because we consider only that which is relevant to the existing way of looking at the situation we can only come back to this existing way. If, however, we could step outside and come in from a different direction then we might be able to generate some new ideas. This effect is shown in Fig. 9 where a new entry point allows one to reach a solution that is perfectly reasonable, once it has been reached.

The second use of PO is to allow one to create new juxtapositions of information that are nowhere to be found in actual experience. For instance, one can introduce a random word that has nothing to do with the problems being considered and then see what happens. PO serves to hold the two separate things together. For example, the problem is to improve the design of a refrigerator:

Random juxtaposition: Refrigerator PO baby

From this unusual context one can go on to various ideas, including development of a small central cooling unit which is then connected by umbilical cords to separate cupboards, each of which can be turned into a refrigerator as required. In one experiment the introduction of a random word in this fashion increased the flow of new ideas fourteenfold.

The basic function of PO is as a de-patterning device. Further ways in which the tool can be used are described in *The Mechanism Of Mind.*

The interesting thing about a device like PO is that it could not have arisen during the normal evolution of language because it is an anti-language word. The function of language is to establish patterns. The function of PO is to facilitate escape from patterns. The concept of PO could only arise from a direct consideration of the behaviour of patterning systems.

PO is a rather extreme example which has been used here simply to indicate that from the consideration of the behaviour of patterning systems one can come up with principles that are quite contrary to the natural development of thinking habits. There are, however, many other practical points that also arise from such a consideration. For instance, most of the basic mistakes of thinking are the direct consequence of the natural behaviour of patterning systems. The important point is that we can at last break away from the circular word games of philosophy to study the behaviour of mind as the functioning of a particular type of information system. We can do this even though we do not yet have all the details of how the brain works. This sort of approach would have been impossible before the development of computers and cybernetics because, from these, the concept of system behaviour has arisen.

Lateral thinking makes good, logical sense if we realise that our minds operate in a universe of patterns. In such a universe de-patterning methods are essential and more than luxuries. If we fail to perceive the patterning nature of perception then lateral thinking remains a bag of tricks. It is a characteristic of science fiction that it sets up a particular universe and asks the reader to accept what becomes logically necessary in that universe. The patterning nature of mind is not a fictitious universe but the most likely one. Nevertheless we first have to look at the universe before understanding the process.

The basic parallelism between lateral thinking and science fiction is that both are *provocative* rather than descriptive or analytical. The very word 'PO' indicates provocation. There may not be a reason for saying something until after it has been said. Once expressed the idea is seen to make sense or to lead to another idea that makes sense. Patterns can only be changed by provocation, not by analysis. Similarly science fiction creates a provocative hypothesis which allows us to look at things in a new way—for our enjoyment or even insight. Because science fiction moves ahead into the future rather than back into the past, it has a total freedom of provocation. The interesting thing about provocation is that it has to be related semi-logically to the existing state of affairs, otherwise it becomes pure gibber-ish which has an annoyance rather than a provocative value. Almost all science fiction situations are PO situations. They offer stepping stones or random juxtapositions in order to excite our interest.

Just as the pattern of our perception is set up by the historical sequence in which images reach our minds so our social and human-behaviour concepts are the results of a sequence of happenings. We often accept the result as inevitable because we can see no alternative. It is true that from within the situation it is difficult to see alternatives. It must be one of the functions of science fiction to move us so far from our own situation that we can see it objectively and can see alternatives. The science fiction themes are not themselves alternatives any more than the PO statements are new ideas or problem solutions. The themes are only provocations or stepping stones. It is the ideas that they provoke in our minds that provide the alternatives.

In science fiction a single change in a particular concept

is often followed through to all its implications. Exactly the same thing happens in lateral thinking. By changing a concept provocatively and following through the change we come to realise that concepts are determined historically rather than by the intrinsic nature of the system. For those who deal with systems it is commonplace to perturb a system in order to study its nature. Those who have no experience of systems still believe that analysis is the only respectable intellectual tool. Both science fiction and lateral thinking are provocative methods. If we dare to think the unthinkable then we may find it easier to think about matters we have always taken for granted.

There is a danger if one forgets that provocative edifices are meant to be provocative and starts to believe in them in their own right. It is always possible to marshal enough rationalising to support anything that is believed in. But that is not the purpose of provocation. The purpose of provocation is to take people on a journey outside of their usual minds—but then to bring them back to the old things seen in a new way.

The tracks described in the piece are the tracks of expectancy —of knowing what things are. Ordinary fiction helps us to know in greater depth and more detail. It strengthens our vision and sensitises our sensitivity but does nothing to change the direction of our vision. Science fiction sets out to do that. So does lateral thinking.

3

Scientific Thought in Fiction and in Fact

JOHN TAYLOR

JOHN TAYLOR

John Taylor is a professor of mathematics at King's College in London. He is best known to the general reading public as the author of several books, including *Black Holes*, and *Super Minds: An Enquiry into the Paranormal*.

I invited him to speak because, as he was working in an area where I knew he was bound to come into conflict with the conservatism of the scientific establishment, I thought that he might be specially sympathetic to one of the most common (and most romantic) preoccupations of modern science fiction: the idea that scientific conservatism may actively work against new ways of seeing the world. Some readers may recall the short story "Noise Level" by Raymond F. Jones, in which a group of scientists is forced by a confidence trick (with government backing) to jettison their world-views. One of them, thus liberated from his preconceptions, goes on to discover antigravity! This story is a convenient archetype of a theme which recurs again and again in science fiction. The theme used to be particularly popular in the SF magazine *Astounding Science Fiction*. It was in this area that I hoped Professor Taylor would talk—as a kind of development of the 'lateral thinking' ideas that Dr de Bono had produced during the previous week's lecture.

In the event it turned out that while Professor Taylor *is* prepared to conduct research in the area of so-called 'fringe' science—an act of some courage for an established scientist— he does not necessarily see science fiction as an automatic ally. His attitude to science fiction—extremely sceptical, though polite and friendly enough—is one I have often met among scientists. It is a useful corrective to the euphoria many SF readers feel as they are swept away, sometimes without sufficient reason, by the apparent intellectual brilliance of their favourite literature.

Professor Taylor's view of science fiction was probably the most controversial—at least with the particular audience he was speaking to—of any expressed during the lecture series.

In this lecture I want to give a scientist's eye view of science fiction and then of science. Let me start by giving you a definition of science fiction. I consider science fiction to be the art of making a scientific 'if' interesting, a scientific 'if' being a postulate or a proposition of scientific form. For example it might be 'if' the wizards of the past were truly effective, or 'if' anti-gravity had been discovered. Such cases can usually be expressed as 'if gravity (or whatever) were different from our present understanding of it'. The 'if' may not in fact be involved with mainstream science. It may have been from science in antiquity, it may be from science of 100 years hence, but it's still a question of making the 'if' interesting. One could call science fiction S.IF, not SF. That is emphasising the 'if' aspect of the work, and of course one has to assume that there's a possibility of the 'if' actually happening. There are many writings which describe ranges of experience which are true fantasy. They are aspects of experience too far from our known world to be met. I think of George Orwell in *1984* as good S.IF, though I suppose when we reach that date it will not be Big Brother but Big Sheikh; his *Animal Farm* is, I think, good fantasy, but fantasy all the same, though sometimes one feels it closer to reality than one would like.

We can recognise various forms of S.IF, but I'm really only going to relate one of them to science and that is the scientific S.IF. For this the scientific 'if' plays a crucial rôle throughout the whole field. H. G. Wells, I think, portrayed this well, as in *The Time Machine*, whose main thread was the change in our understanding and so control of time, enabling one to travel backwards and forwards in it. At the time of its writing there weren't the scientific possibilities open that have been more recently realised, for example by the black hole and other features of the curvature of space and time; however, the story certainly was in the stream of scientific thought of its own time.

Another type of science fiction is space opera; James Blish's *Cities in Flight* is one example of that, one that's quite appealing (for example, it would be nice to have London in the Mediterranean right now). In space opera little importance is attached to the scientific aspects of the chosen 'if'; we can truly say that the operatic aspects of the plot are emphasised.

Finally there is whimsical S.IF, where the scientific aspect is completely played down. I don't think it's relevant and is only remotely related to science, though of course it is enjoyable.

Scientific ideas in scientific S.IF cover an enormous range. Naturally enough any possible scientific ideas, any possible scientific law is fair game to be thought of as being broken. I've already mentioned time travel in Wells's *Time Machine*, and anti-gravity, for example in Blish's *Earthman, Come Home*. There's a vast amount of S.IF on telepathy, such as Colin Wilson's *The Mind Parasites*, a good example in that it's so relevant to modern research in telepathy and its related area of distant viewing. Longevity, perpetual motion—there are many, many themes: in fact, all ranges of possible scientific laws; our common sense, which is governed by these laws, can be violated, and the interesting features of this for human experience then explored.

There are many more examples. But the crucial point to realise in so much of this S.IF is that it is not relevant to fundamental science. The problems that are tackled by science fiction writers are not ones that really are of great interest to the legitimate scientist. This is clear when we contrast S.IF, the making a scientific 'if' interesting from the human point of view, with what I would regard as the essentials of science. In that latter I see the basic feature as the question of testing the way the world works. It is the correctness of that 'if' that is the point here. It might be terribly tedious in proving the correctness, but the essential feature that is important here is that it is so. It is a completely opposite emphasis to S.IF, since in science one cannot choose one's 'if' as one likes. The external world seems to do that for us.

Examples of this, and very famous ones, are Newton's laws of motion and his inverse square law of gravity. Newton's three laws of motion describe the motion of particles, and the question is whether, with an inverse square law of gravity and Newton's laws of motion, one gets the correct motion of the planets. There are many predictions that follow from these two basic hypotheses. There are therefore many good tests of these ideas, and indeed for 200 years or more they were found satisfactory. Then came the developments of 1900 or so leading to relativity, to do with the curvature of space and time. Newton's laws and the inverse square law of gravity were found unsatisfactory, and so the ifs that were postulated had to be changed to further ifs.

Again, however, there was a strictly limited range of possibilities. Scientists just can't play crossword puzzles. I think that is the moral to draw from any scientific exercise. You can't choose the rules of the game according to the way you feel at the time, or the way you think your readers will like best. That is one of the basic problems of science today, and possibly a feature that prevents children from coming into science in as great numbers as they used to. (There are other reasons for this, naturally enough, to do with pollution, and all the other things that science is blamed for.) But the feeling is, I think, quite strong that science is out of one's control, that you cannot play with it just as you would like, that you have to fit in with the way the world works, not fit it in to the way you work. This feature is something that for some people, at least, is unsatisfactory: they can't 'do their own thing'. There are restrictions in science that make a vast difference between science fiction (S.IF in particular) and science. S.IF is perhaps so attractive because it *lacks* restrictions.

As I have emphasised, we can't get away from such a lack of choice in science. This is related to the conservatism of science, which is often attacked as being full of old fuddy-duddies who will not change their ideas nor accept new ideas coming in. For example somebody suggests an anti-gravity device, or someone says that special relativity is wrong. Such a person, who may come in and attempt to overthrow established science, because it does not fit his ideas, does not appreciate what it is he's overthrowing—how much success he is prepared to reject. And this is, of course, the reason that scientists hold on so firmly and conservatively to what they have achieved, except where it can be shown that there is some better way of achieving what they have got already and of going even further.

There are many cases in point where this advance has

happened. But such advances do not occur without a big rear-guard action being fought by some scientists, and indeed the battles can be very unpleasant. I've been in the heart of some of them, seen the knives out and sensed the emotions; I've noticed the people who will not speak to each other for many years afterwards. This still persists; such wars will recur because scientists are only human. But they are also scientific in wishing to hold on to a world that they feel is something they understand.

An example of this is the present idea of the uncertain nature of matter, usually called 'the uncertainty principle': that the position and velocity of a particle cannot be specified with arbitrary accuracy. This vagueness was something that could not be accepted by certain scientists. Even today there is a battle going on as to whether it works properly or not, stimulated very much by the philosophical and metaphysical leanings of the scientists involved.

Einstein said that God would not play dice with the world, even though he started the destruction of Newtonian certainty with his original paper on the photoelectric effect, for which he got a Nobel prize. He still fought against the mathematical formulations of the uncertainty principle in the wave mechanics of the 1920s, and he died a lonely man, having worked for the last 30 years of his life trying to change establishment science right outside the mainstream of scientific development of his time. I think that he was a scientist who did not appreciate the successes of the science then current.

People coming in from outside who claim that they have better ideas than scientists must learn science first, before they come and challenge the scientists and say, 'I can do better than you'. They might indeed be able to do it in one small area, but it might be a very *ad hoc* approach, just applying to that restricted area and not relevant to the whole of the remaining successful range of scientific experience.

I want to illustrate this point with changes that do have enormous effects on science, although science fiction writers and many people on the fringes of science seem to think that the basic ideas of modern science can be modified without much of a problem. A phenomenon which, if true, would bring such a change about is the materialisation of objects, an event which for some people is fairly straightforward! I was invited by 'phone just recently, for example, to go to a greengrocer's in South London. At eleven o'clock every Wednesday morning, I was told, fertilizer materialises from the roof. Now I felt that I didn't particularly want to stand around with the fertilizer materialising from the roof and falling on me. It didn't seem to be the most helpful sort of thing to have happen, even if I had an umbrella. It was so outside my range of scientific understanding and comprehension, and so unlikely to be occurring, that in a sense I was a little close-minded about this. If you ask the really hard scientist, he will say 'rubbish, impossible, somebody is faking it', and indeed somebody would have to do so, when you consider the remarkable amount of energy that would be required to achieve such effects. If one wants to materialise or de-materialise a spoon, something that I've seen a lot of this last year, the energy and information required to cause it to appear again inside a closed box, for example, can be roughly calculated, and it is astronomical. It seems impossible to achieve such effects by normal human means. We would have to throw away most of our scientific understanding to think of any explanation. Hence, one holds on to the scientific explanation, and doesn't look too closely inside closed boxes.

Time travel is another S.IF that, as I said, H. G. Wells started off with. It is an attractive idea, but if we accept it then there are going to be difficulties with the bases of science; the scientific community therefore tends to reject this possibility. Most scientific ifs in S.IF involve an aspect of experience that would become so contradictory to standard science that it would be overthrown and we would be left in a very naked state, scientifically speaking.

The changes in our outlook on life produced by change in the fundamental scientific ideas are numerous. One still continuing example began back in 1919, when general relativity caught the public fancy and was on everybody's lips for months. This was the time when the ideas of Einstein had been verified by the observed bending of light by the sun, and a public debate on the curvature of time and space began.

Let me try and summarise these points about the relationship of science and science fiction, and in particular S.IF, by claiming that there is no relevance in S.IF to fundamental science. S.IF discusses the implications of the breakdown of whatever scientific law is chosen, which are not, however, usually carried right through—possibly because they are not relevant to the story, but very often, I feel, because the science fiction writer has himself not appreciated how damaging his idea is to the superstructure of science that has been so laboriously created over hundreds of years.

On the positive side, S.IF has some relevance to technology. Arthur C. Clarke is one of the foremost S.IF writers to show this. Space travel is obviously a promising phenomenon of the future. The relevance of S.IF to the social impact of science is, I think, even higher. For example *The Andromeda Strain* has a very close parallel to the present problems of genetic engineering, with the recently suggested moratorium on changing the genetic structure of viruses in case one such was developed which would be fatal to the human race.

I think that even more important is the inspirational feature of S.IF. I myself would say that this is maybe its most important rôle. For example, Isaac Asimov has written that he considers that it is very good for students to have an early experience of science fiction, even in school, to arouse their interest in science. I would agree with this; it is quite clear that this has already had a useful effect. But I think there is more to it than that. For the mature among us it has the great value of opening our horizons—'mind-boggling', in brief.

However, we should also recognise that some areas of science are even more conjectural than science fiction, and indeed I think S.IF is not necessarily more brave, more exciting. There are far more 'mind-boggling' features going on in science (and many more *Brave New World* aspects) now than ever in the past, possibly excepting the time of the cultural heyday in Ancient Greece. It would seem that science is now ahead of science fiction and is writing the science fiction scenario for the future. And this is so in spite of the limitations imposed on science, of taking nature as it comes and not changing it out of all recognition. To have stolen a march on science fiction under such conditions is remarkable indeed.

To show this, let me spend a little time talking about the mysteries of modern science. We now realise that 15,000 million years ago, there was a big bang and the cosmic egg, sitting there for no apparent reason, blew up. Why it blew up is the second mystery (the first being why it was there). Since that auspicious start, galaxies formed from the expanding matter and then stars were formed from local condensation of those galaxies, all under the effects of gravity attracting the bits of matter together that were flying apart.

The stars themselves contracted more and heated up in their centres; by fusion reactions these stars go through a reasonably stable period of life, sometimes, hopefully, for billions of years, so allowing life to develop. Ultimately a star such as our sun will end up, having finished burning up all its nuclear fuel, as a white dwarf dying away in a graceful old age. It would not be very large, about the size of the earth: quite dense, but certainly not in any catastrophic fashion. But if a star is a little heavier, about 1·2 times the sun's mass, then it is in difficulty, because there is too much attraction between its parts to hold itself up. It can either end up as a neutron star which is seen as a pulsar —or alternatively, if it is a bit heavier than twice the sun's mass, it will end up as a black hole.

This black hole—a collapsing star—is a very strange object, certainly stranger than anything predicted in science fiction, and something that right now is presenting the greatest paradox and the greatest difficulty to science. This is, that the very laws that indicate the black hole should be formed are themselves destroyed at its centre. This is because of the gravitational forces that are squeezing the collapsing star ever smaller as it gets more compressed. Suppose you were sitting on the surface of such a star as it was collapsing. Your escape velocity would increase and increase until it would ultimately reach the velocity of light. But when the escape velocity becomes equal to that of light then the size of the object is critical, and at that point you cannot get off. That is, assuming you cannot go faster than light.

This latter limitation is another area where there has been much conjecture in science fiction, where it is often assumed that one can indeed go faster than light, but some of the paradoxes presented by that idea have not been fully appreciated. Scientists in the last decade have considered very seriously particles that do go faster than light. They have been given the name tachyons, from the Greek 'tachis', meaning swift. Tachyons have been looked for, and every now and again somebody claims to have discovered them. I'm afraid that at present the evidence is that they do not exist.

If they did exist, we would be in trouble because we could signal back into our past. I could, for example, signal back into my past and prevent my mother and father from meeting, and I do not then see how I could give this talk here tonight. It would be an embarrassment for the scientists concerned if tachyons existed; it certainly would destroy causality. Scientific method as we know it would not actually work if tachyons existed. But that does not stop experimenters going to look for them; in fact, they'd be very happy to find them, and would say, 'Well, you guys were all wrong in the first place, weren't you?' But tachyons haven't been found. We have to accept, as of now, that if you sat on a collapsing star ultimately you would never be able to get off. And that is the reason that these objects are called 'black holes': they absorb things that fall into them, but nothing can get out again because it would have to travel faster than light to do so.

The size of the star for which the escape velocity at its surface is equal to that of light has reached a critical point which it is natural to call an event horizon; you can't see what goes on inside it. All is absorbed that falls inside the event horizon: a black hole is the best garbage can you can think of. The trouble is it becomes bigger as you put more rubbish into it, so you have to step back a pace each time, but that is something one can always do.

A black hole is a strange enough object, but what happens inside at its very centre is what is now causing problems. Inside the event horizon, matter will fall to the centre in a finite amount of time. If you were sitting on the surface of a collapsing star, reading your wristwatch, it would take you a ten-thousandth of a second to fall to the centre if the collapsing object was about ten times the sun's mass. After that time you would have become of zero size.

After a finite amount of time, infalling matter vanishes. This is very disturbing. Our scientific equations can't describe that; our laws break down. The act of vanishing is not part of the rule book of present-day physics. This is a bigger difficulty than we have had in the last 70 years of science. We don't know any way out of it right now, and it's very embarrassing to admit almost complete defeat: we presently still have hopes of avoiding it, otherwise we would not continue to work on the subject. Hopefully we will find out how to change the laws we have and how to make it a sensible world, right to the centre of the black hole.

It is interesting that you cannot actually publish what goes on inside a black hole unless you fall inside it, and then the publication time is rather short. It may be, of course, a good way to prevent too much in the way of publication, but I think it's the hard way of going about it. There seems no solution to this destruction of the 'consensibility' criterion of science, once inside an event horizon; it has even been suggested that what happens inside it can be completely neglected as considered from the outside. That is clearly the coward's way out.

There may also be what are called 'naked singularities' that don't have an event horizon around them. We can actually see from a distance what is happening as matter vanishes at the centre of one of these. If a naked singularity did exist, it would be difficult to say what precisely it looked like, since we do not know how to describe matter in this very compressed state.

That is the bad news about gravity, but there is the good news about the other forces of nature. Our understanding of these other forces is in quite a good state. There are three of them; the force of electromagnetism, the nuclear force holding particles together inside the nucleus, and the force of radio-activity.

The force of electromagnetism is the one which basically controls chemistry, since it is the force holding electrons orbiting around a nucleus, and not really dependent on what happens inside the nucleus. The nuclear force holds the particles together inside the nucleus, and we think we understand more now about the laws of attraction between two protons, or a proton and a neutron. Radio-activity is the other force, the third force of nature, which causes uranium, for example, to decay into lead.

We think we can now unify these three forces together in a universe which includes uncertainty. This latter is a basic feature of the world which has to be accepted, involving as it does only the probability, but not the certainty, of finding an electron a certain distance from a nucleus. The electron is smeared out around the nucleus, so to say. This probabilistic feature of the world is something we can build into the three forces of nature. We now have a theory of these forces which is consistent with the probabilistic nature of matter and we can go down to 10^{-15} of a centimetre with this theory, without contradiction with observation. This success is not only remarkable but it is also rather depressing, since we would like to have the theory break down sooner or later. For only in that way can a better theory be developed and the old one explained.

The three forces of nature have, in fact, been unified in the last few years, and the two or three new elementary particles that have been discovered in the last few months are a possible indication that the unification is succeeding.

It is a sad state of affairs that gravity does not fit in with the probabilistic nature of matter. It is that problem that we face when we are at the centre of a black hole in compressed matter; at that critical moment we have to take account of gravity and the other three forces of matter simultaneously. Thus we have to develop a unified theory in which we have one super force, hopefully in a super world. Only then can we expect to resolve the paradox of the vanishing of matter at the centre of a black hole.

Whilst we are in a relatively good state of affairs about the outer world, except for gravity, what about the inner world? That's a much more difficult problem, especially as we have got at least 300 years of leeway to catch up in understanding what goes on inside us, in comparison with what goes on outside. It was only about 1800 or so that we began to have any detailed understanding of the brain and the way it controls behaviour. If we look at this problem from the hard scientist's point of view, we see that we can get a reasonable understanding of the whole range of phenomena in the brain from looking at its detailed working.

The trouble with the brain is that it is a very complicated organ which doesn't look at all complex. It is composed of regions which have different functional importance. For example there are various regions in the cortex that are to do with control of the various senses, vision and so on. There are also vast regions of the cortex in which we don't know quite what is happening. This may be the origin of the old folklore story, that if you could only use that extra nine-tenths of the brain you'd be very well off. But if you actually did so you would be very badly off, because if we understand it right, the extra nine-tenths of the brain is certainly not there for fun, but relates the primary visual, the primary sensory and all the other areas together.

The body is represented in quite a detailed way on the surface of the motor and sensory cortex, the areas controlling movement and sensory perception. One can tell by the way an animal's body is represented on the surface of its cortex, in fact, what the animal is most interested in doing.

What is done in brain research to find out how the brain does control behaviour is to put electrodes in various animals' brains and see what happens when you put current into those electrodes in different regions. A cat, for example, might be caused to lift its hind paw by electrode stimulation in a particular region of its cortex. It is interesting to note that if too much electrode current is put in while the cat is dropped, it can't actually pull the final leg down; it just cannot overcome that current, and does not seem to have any free will about it. There are numerous epileptic patients who have had electrodes implanted in their brains. They can then be 'turned off' if they start to have an epileptic seizure. There are numbers of patients who have to be dealt with in this way because they've committed murder or some other crime, unexpectedly, due to a past brain injury. With the present large number of car accidents, there are increasing numbers of people who may at some time in the future suddenly go berserk and kill their nearest and dearest. Better understanding of brain function will ameliorate such situations.

When you ask, 'How does the brain work?', you have to look at the cellular structure in detail. The brain is composed of billions of single nerve cells, and the problem is, how do those billions work together? Though it has not been solved yet, there are vigorous attempts being made. Discovering how the connections are working, and discovering how they might achieve success in the way we think, leads us into a very technical area. Great care is necessary, since a single nerve cell on its own may have ten thousand or even a quarter of a million other nerve cells connecting to it.

A single nerve cell has buttons on its surface from all the other nerve cells that are sending their information to that single cell. What is going on at the gaps, or the synapses as they are called, at these junctions from one nerve cell to the next, is very crucial, especially to the understanding of memory. Just before the synaptic gaps are little spheres that are called vesicles. It is these which are thought to cause the transmission of information from one cell to the next. It is interesting to realise that memory has been brought down to a level of this sort. Each vesicle may contain several thousand molecules and will float into the synaptic gap and across it to cause the next cell to be activated. An appreciation of that is, I think, very crucial to understanding what is going on in brain research.

A very basic problem in brain research, in fact you might say *the* most basic one is: What is the mind? Is it something that extends right outside ourselves? Or is it really inside the skull? That is the problem that is not properly faced up to by modern brain research, though some workers are attempting to build generalised animals that might have higher levels of conscious-ness than ourselves. The point is that one has to have a pro-gramme which can ultimately explain the mind. A number of people working in brain research themselves would say that is impossible; they would say you could never describe the internal world in physical terms. In fact, from a philosophical point of view, it is possible that we may be able to build a consistent model which will join the metaphysical ethos to the materialist ethos. There even appear to be ways of constructing, at least in principle, machines that might have much more powerful minds than our own. I might add that as far as I know no S.IF writer has ever suggested any way of constructing a machine which has a mind as capable as our own. I think this supports the point that I made earlier, that S.IF is not relevant to fundamental research.

Let me now turn to ESP, which has been claimed as an indication that there are some severe restrictions on any theory of the mind that is presently put forward. For example, let us consider levitation. It seems impossible, yet has been observed by some, apparently, under conditions which did not allow fraud. The paranormal is an area that has not been very wel-come in established science for a number of reasons. There is a

whole range of other abnormal phenomena to consider: telepathy, distant viewing, psycho-kinesis, spoon-bending, messages
from the dead, materialisation and many more.

The early work of scientists in this area was somewhat
biased. They knew in advance what they wanted, they knew in
advance what the answers should be, and this deficiency in
objectivity has been clear to establishment science. Further-
more, if ESP were true it would seem to destroy too much of
science for a scientist to accept. I know of scientists, some very
good ones, who have refused to be present at demonstrations of
ESP, saying that they would rather not see it, whatever it was,
because this might destroy their world.

I sympathise with them; in fact, after I'd seen Uri Geller, I
spent a couple of pretty difficult days trying to sort out my
ideas as to how this phenomenon could be achieved, whether by
fraud or not. I think that sort of 'soul-searching' is very good
for one. Finally there is always the question of fraud, one
that has to be taken very seriously. Since it has abounded so
much in ESP in the past it has given the subject a very bad
name.

I suppose the central reason why science has shied away from
ESP is the question of getting data which are reproducible.
People will come back with eye-witness accounts of ESP tests
and say, 'I've seen this, I've seen that,' and other people will
then ask, well, can we go and see it also? They will try to do so
and in most cases fail. The data don't appear to be reproducible,
a *sine qua non* as far as scientific investigation is concerned.

Naturally enough, this lack of support for ESP from established science, due to lies, fraud and lack of reproducibility, has
meant that there is little financial help towards research in
this area. Certainly there is no support from any established
scientific body. In fact I was personally turned down by a
national fund-giving body with the response, 'What would
happen if there was a question asked in the House of Commons
about the use of scientific funds in this area?'

I have myself been investigating most extensively the problem
of spoon-bending, a phenomenon best publicised by Uri Geller,
the Israeli. I've tested him, and a number of children who have
also proved successful at spoon-bending, and I've found the
phenomenon occurring under conditions in which there was no

chance of fraud. There are also other groups of scientists in this country, and throughout the world, who are investigating the many people that have come forward with such powers. There are the problems of repeatability here, as in other areas of ESP, but they do not seem to be insurmountable. The subjects can repeat their spoon-bending feats quite often, though a great deal of patience is required in working with them. If the problem as to how it happens can be solved then, who knows, a new chapter may well be written in science. It is a really good challenge, just as good as the centre of the black hole. It is certainly a very exciting time to live in science.

I want to close by saying that I see the main purpose of science fiction as allowing the majority of us who do not work in science, and who do not see this excitement except from newspaper reports, to appreciate the fact that the world is rapidly changing. It is a way of taking account of future shock, a way of 'boggling your mind' once a day or once a week. That is a feature that scientists have to face up to every time they start out on a problem. Every day one may read in a scientific journal or in a letter, or hear by telephone, of an experiment that shatters the particular world view that a scientist is working from. This happened only a few months ago with the discovery of two new particles, completely unexpected. That sort of possibility is a feature we all learn to live with in science, and it is one that I think we're having to learn to cope with much more in the modern world. I would say that science fiction serves its purpose if it achieves this much for *all* of us. If it enables each and every one of us to be less conservative in our outlook, and be ready to envisage alternative existences which may be quite different from our present one, then it will perform a great service for us. If science fiction could, at the same time, indicate clearly the need to clarify the pitfalls of these alternatives before we embark on one or other of them it would be even more valuable. Indeed I would recommend such an approach as a part of the school curriculum. Let me finish by wishing you success in finding the best of your alternative futures.

4

Science Fiction and the Larger Lunacy

JOHN BRUNNER

JOHN BRUNNER

John Brunner has distinguished himself in two ways as a science fiction writer: as the very readable and efficient author of a great many quite light-weight science fiction 'entertainments', and as the author of a smaller number of longer and more serious novels, most of them (like *Stand on Zanzibar*, *The Jagged Orbit* and *The Sheep Look Up*) devoted to investigating the likely problems of the near future.

When I asked John to speak, I knew that he had just finished working on a novel (*The Shockwave Rider*, now published) which is based in part on the sociological and economic theories of Alvin Toffler, who was to speak himself later on in the series. I had supposed that John would prefer to speak on 'Science Fiction and the Problems of the Future', or some similar subject, but I gave him a free choice, and to my surprise the subject he came up with was not, as I had expected, a companion piece to Alvin Toffler's, but instead, a companion piece (unintentionally so) to John Taylor's.

I remain amused at the irony that it was a science fiction writer (a breed widely supposed by the cynical public to be especially susceptible to every 'fringe' science theory which comes along) who produced the heavy assault on the 'fringe' sciences, while it was the pure scientist who was investigating them. (Though I must be fair, and point out that Brunner's attack is *not* specifically on those areas of fringe science being investigated by Professor Taylor.)

John Brunner has what an American once described to me, admiringly it must be said, as 'a posh English accent'. He also has an apparently self-confident lecturing manner. This blend, I knew well, nearly always succeeds in goading a part of his audience into fury, and John's lectures are often followed by a fiery question period. This time, though, the audience (or 95 per cent of it) was very obviously in total agreement with him—an interesting fact I offer to any young sociologist who is about to make an ass of himself by announcing that science fiction fans are notoriously weak-minded about scientific rigour, and particularly prone to fall for whatever the latest cult theory happens to be.

*Dedicated to all those people
who, in the immortal words of L. Sprague de Camp,
'never having had an original idea themselves,
find it impossible to imagine anybody else's
having one . . .'*

Here to start with are a couple of stern injunctions which have recently turned up in my morning mail. The first is a small-ad culled from Andy Porter's magazine *Algol,* and it delivers the following warning:

ATTENTION: People Of Earth: Unless you immediately cease all racism, sexism, ageism, totalitarianism, wars of aggression, cruelty to animals, vivisection, environmental rape, abortion and euthanasia, you will receive no further contact from us, THE GALACTIC SOCIETY. For further information, have your leader contact FEMINISTS FOR LIFE

. . . which you can do, by the way, via a post office box in Columbus, Ohio.

One has an awful suspicion that this advertisement is seriously intentioned: that the person who inserted it does honestly expect a higher proportion of SF fans than of the general public to put $1 in an envelope in order to obtain a copy of *Sisterlife Proceedings: First International Prolife Feminist Conference.* (I predict the advertisers will be disappointed, and that an exceptionally high proportion of SF readers will identify the phraseology as indicating a right-wing, probably Catholic or fundamentalist, front organisation, and save their money. Of course, I could very well be wrong.)

But one did hope that over the past couple of decades the

attitude of non-SF people towards SF types might have altered just a little . . . Oh, maybe it was always too much to expect. It certainly hasn't happened in other areas. Twenty-some years ago, on the cover of Walter Willis's fanzine *Hyphen*, appeared a two-drawing cartoon which showed, first, some SF fans queueing in high excitement among a bunch of bored Sunday-afternooners at a cinema advertising a science fiction film; and second, the fans coming out again with faces long as fiddles while everybody else is beaming, overjoyed.

Anyone who has seen *Zardoz*, to name but a few, must be painfully aware how little has changed on that level. The appearance of this advertisement suggests that the same is true in other connections.

My second example, which is somewhat more succinct, is a slogan franked on an envelope posted in Philadelphia, and says: 'SUPPORT YOUR LOCAL SORCERER'. Indeed I shall! Let the gentleman in question but appeal to me, and I swear I'll cross his palm with cupronickel.

So far, so fair enough. We are in the context of a familiar tradition. In the heyday of the science fiction (and other) pulps, advertisements could be found at the back of the magazines for just about everything from pimple-creams to pistols. Not infrequently the secret of the universe was on offer at 49¢ plus post and packing. It was almost as though the various nutters automatically thought, 'Who's even more out of his gourd than I am?' And, catching sight of a copy of *Amazing*, or *Astounding*, or *Thrilling Wonder* . . .

And, at around the same time, when Lovecraft and his associates were elaborating the Cthulhu mythos, they built a series of private jokes into their cosmos. Not all were as transparent as the one which incarnated Clark Ashton Smith as 'Klarkash-Ton'; none the less (and who could expect otherwise in a coterie that included Robert Bloch?) a redeeming element of wit kept cropping up in those turgid tales.

Transformed a trifle, our parameters remain recognisable. But——!

But coexistent with these harmless varieties of spinoff from identifiable predecessors there is something else, which often causes me to lie awake brooding into the small hours. The phenomenon I have in mind is, in many people's view, inextricably associated with SF, and one can scarcely deny that SF has contributed to it; at the height of *Amazing*'s success in the late 1940s, when the 'Shaver Mystery' had boosted its circulation to an incredible 300,000 copies per month, editor Ray Palmer used to interrupt conversations with visiting fans and dive under his desk to avoid attacks by the evil doers, the survivors of lost Lemuria. Equally, one is obliged to recall the Dean Drive, dianetics, the Hieronymus Machine . . .

And yet, in some hard-to-pin-down way, this phenomenon has always been *foreign* to SF. A case in point: when, one year, the World SF Convention in America found itself sharing the hotel with a convention of Scientologists, many of the latter assumed (because of Hubbard's connection with the SF magazines in the 'forties and 'fifties) that fans would be easy targets for Scientology propaganda. In the upshot, the grapevine later reported that the main contact between the two conventions occurred on Saturday night when a number of SF fans found a back way into the Scientologists' dance-hall and took advantage of their band and their bar. The bridge convention which clashed with the SF Con at Washington in 1974 did slightly better in that respect. I was told that two couples who had come for the SF Con changed their minds and spent the weekend playing bridge instead.

Generally speaking, we in the SF community have the common decency to remind people as often as it proves necessary that what we are trading in *is* fiction.

But there are a frightening number of people in positions of far greater influence and authority than any among our enclosed in-group, who are either unable or—more likely, in my view—unwilling to emphasise this distinction. Loss of the faculty to discriminate between the real and the unreal, between sensory datum and hallucination, is perhaps the single most significant criterion by which one defines the onset of insanity. What one is to make of people who simply disregard the difference . . . I don't know. That's why I get insomnia. It is as though this species of ours is in the process of losing either the gift of reason which our ancestors declared was what set us apart from the brute creation, or the pleasure which formerly could be derived by exercising it.

Let me quote the small-ad preceding the one I've already cited. It reflects what to my mind is a real threat. Even though this adumbration of it is exceptionally (I would say deceptively) naïve, I am afraid we are confronted by the symptoms of a sort of mass psychosis. The advertisement runs:

> NEED someone who can create a new church, based on a combination of Velikovsky, Heinlein, Rand, and optimistic futurology. An active, live-wire promoter is needed and compensation will have to come from the results as no cash is available. Charter and tax exemption already arranged. Church of the New Revelation

—*Incorporated*, of course! And I suspect it will come as no surprise to some among us to learn that the return address of this church is in New Jersey.

Now catching sight of that advertisement called back to memory a book I must first have read when I was eight or nine and which I admire so much I've managed to keep hold of it; it has a place of honour in my present study. Consulting it, I located the following passage:

> . . . self-worship and State-worship are within the reach of all.
>
> A third possibility is the rise on the ruins of Christianity of a religion with a creed in harmony with modern thought, or more probably the thought of a generation ago.
>
> . . . The old religions are full of outworn science, including the astronomical theory of a solid heaven, the chemical theory that water, bread, books, and other objects can be rendered holy by special processes, and the physiological theory that a substance called a soul leaves the body at the moment of death. I remember hearing a former headmaster of Eton informing the school from the pulpit that the body lost weight (or gained it, I forget which) at the moment of death . . . A new religion would probably include in its creed the reality of the ether, the habitability of Mars, the duty of man to co-operate in the process of evolution,

the existence of innate psychological difference between the human races, and the wickedness of either capitalism or socialism.

No wonder that advertisement for the Church of the New Revelation—*Inc.*—sounded curiously familiar. What was the recipe for its creation...? Ah, yes: 'optimistic futurology' blended with Rand, Heinlein and Velikovsky.

So let's just check off the correspondences, shall we? It seems fair enough, for instance, to suggest that man's co-operation in the process of evolution would fulfil the wildest dreams of our optimistic futurologists, some of whom are optimistic enough to disregard natural laws when those happen to conflict with their ambitions for humanity.

I scarcely need to explain, I think, which out of the pair capitalism/socialism Ayn Rand regards as wholly evil. (No marks to anybody who assumed that 'Rand' meant the Rand Corporation, and even fewer for those who took it as being a South African monetary unit.)

And although pseudo-scientific *Rassenwissenschaft* may not be as fashionable or as obligatory as when one of the wisest men of our century pondered the possibility of new religions, there are still among us pundits who, instead of regarding ethnic differences as evidence of the vigour, vitality and variety of mankind—qualities, in sum, to be welcomed and encouraged—treat them as proof of some hierarchical system of 'superiority' and 'inferiority'. Not only do their arguments always tend to demonstrate that the group they were born into is the Top Type; they compound their offence by equating this alleged superiority with the ability to inflict destruction on their fellow beings. The Nazis and their 'race-scientists' may have gone to the oubliette. We are still burdened with too many arrogant fools who regard themselves as an ideal towards which all mankind is obliged to strive.

As to habitability of Mars: where else did Heinlein send Valentine Michael Smith (*Stranger in a Strange Land*) to spend his formative years? And as to the existence of 'the ether' ...

Well, when trying to authenticate Joshua's instruction to the sun to stand still, Velikovsky ran into a minor difficulty. He

had the kinetic energy of the rotation of our planet to get rid of
—on a temporary basis, because it came back within a very
short while—without (as Asimov has astutely observed)
breaking those stalactites and stalagmites in limestone caverns
which have been a-building for millennia and are even yet
so fragile your incautious elbow can snap them off. This is on
top of the need to avoid melting the Earth's crust.

So Velikovsky, in *Worlds in Collision*, invoked a medium to
transfer that energy in the form of colossal lightning-flashes
from Earth to, and back again from, comet-Venus. It is only
fair to emphasise that (to my knowledge) the term 'ether' has
not been applied by Velikovsky himself. However, one is
tempted to imagine that some of his followers must have
learned their 'physics' from Alfred Jarry's *Telepathic Letter to
Lord Kelvin*. ('Pataphysics is THE science ... but nobody is
disputing that!)

What have we here? Something approaching a one-to-one
fit!

The man who was able so exactly to outline the form a new
religion would take, even after his own death, was J. B. S.
Haldane. I wish I knew when he wrote the piece I have quoted,
"Science and Theology"; unfortunately I can only say that the
copy of his essay-collection *Possible Worlds* which I possess is
dated 1940 and it must therefore have been written some time
in the 'thirties or perhaps even the 'twenties.

Am I misguided in my reaction to that small-ad which did,
after all, appear in a magazine of limited circulation, and—as
I said before—is amazingly naïve?

Well, to quote my favourite authority, Anon., 'even paranoids
have real enemies'.

Consider these excerpts from an article by the distinguished
Indian writer Ved Mehta, which appeared in the London
Observer on 19 January 1975:

> I've been visiting India every year for many years now.
> Each year, fear, corruption, and violence have increased, but
> this year they seem to have become a way of life ...
> Old accounts of Indian intrigue, nepotism, and courts and

courtiers written by European observers in the eighteenth and early nineteenth centuries bear an unnerving resemblance to what is happening now. Signs of backward-looking political and religious nationalism are everywhere . . . There is constant talk about the glories of ancient India—about how the Hindus in Vedic times travelled around in flying machines, talked to each other on 'skyphones', and constructed 'bridges of stones' spanning oceans. The heroic feats and the anthropomorphic characteristics of the *devas*, or gods, and *asuras*, or demons, in the ancient Hindu epics are being taken literally again. The foreign book most widely discussed among students at Delhi University is Erich von Däniken's 'Chariots of the Gods'. The students take it as proof that in antiquity not only India but also other parts of the world lived through a technological age more advanced than that to be found in the West today.

One had been accustomed to expect that India, with her rich history and vast population, would become one of the great nations of the twenty-first century, wielding power and exerting influence commensurate with her magnificent heritage. Instead, it is infinitely saddening to be told that her best minds are falling under the sway of a pseudo-scientific charlatan.

Some may regard that as excessively strong language. I disagree. If anything, it is over-temperate. Consider the following remarks by the head of the department of Semitic studies at the University of Sydney, Australia. He is talking about a subject he is well acquainted with, the tombs of the Valley of the Kings in Egypt, and reviewing von Däniken's claims about them.

Light in the Tombs
Von Däniken points out that the painting of large areas of wall inside dark passages constitutes a problem for him. He states, quite correctly, that there are no signs of carbon from any sort of lamp or flare, and that electricity was unknown to the ancient Egyptians (quite irreconcilably, he states that the remains of an electric battery was found in Mesopotamia). He consequently concludes that the astronauts must have introduced to the ancient Egyptians some other form of

artificial illumination; but if he were to travel to Luxor today I could introduce him to a septuagenarian dragoman Ahmed Yahya who has taken me into the inmost recesses of tombs in the Valley of the Kings, perfectly illumined without the aid of artificial lighting. Sheets of polished metal placed at given places along the passageways reflect the rays of the sun so perfectly, and the placing of these 'mirrors' is so skilfully arranged, that electric lighting is unnecessary.

Von Däniken's chief weakness is sheer ignorance

—Hear, hear! I wish I'd been the first to say that!—

thus he states that the island of Elephantine in the Nile is so called because it resembles an elephant in shape, and that this can only be recognized from an aeroplane as there is no hill in the vicinity from which this can be seen. This ignores several facts: 1. the word *elephantinos* in Greek does not mean *elephant;* it means *ivory* and is a translation of Egyptian *Yeb,* a name which goes back to very early times (it would appear that the island of Yeb may anciently have been a place where ivory was bought from elephant-hunters who brought it down stream). 2. The hill upon which the Aga Khan's tomb is built overlooks the island which bears no resemblance to the shape of an elephant, a fact supported by maps. This does not, of course, make allowance for the probability that the shape of the island has almost certainly changed over the millennia; in which· case von Däniken's pretended modern confirmation of his claims falls to the ground.

Similarly von Däniken claims that Egyptian mummification was an art imparted to the inhabitants of the Nile Valley by astronauts who knew how to restore the dead to life. Such a statement ignores the fact that sophistication in methods of mummification developed in Egypt over a long period, and it is possible to trace and set out how this took place, step by step. It began with observation of the simple fact that a body left in desert areas will desiccate and, unless destroyed by animals, will last almost indefinitely . . . thus in Australia the desiccated bodies of persons lost in desert country have been known to survive for many years. The Egyptians aided this process by removing those parts of the body in which bacteria normally dwell `and which, when death inhibits the production of protecting secretions by the body, attack their former home. The removal of viscera and brain can scarcely have been considered by von Däniken's highly scientific astronauts as conducive to revival of a dead body.

Is is not a shameful reflection upon our society—perhaps our entire species—that whereas you have heard about, and very possibly read, the works of Erich von Däniken, the odds are enormous against your identifying the book from which I drew that quotation?

Its title is *Some Trust in Chariots* (Thiering and Castle, eds: Popular Library, 1972), and it's an Australian symposium of essays exposing von Däniken's grosser falsehoods. My personal favourite is the piece by a civil engineer named Clive Houlsby, who corrects such weirdly inaccurate statements by von Däniken as the claim that the blocks used for the pyramids weigh twelve tons (they average out about $2\frac{1}{2}$ tons) and that the ancient Egyptians were ignorant of rope (not only are quantities of it on show in various museums but there are rope-making scenes painted on the walls of fifth dynasty tombs) and ultimately shoots von Däniken down in flames with this short but devastating comment: 'His [von Däniken's] offer of his kingdom for a convincing explanation of the transport of the stone blocks is accepted with gusto!'

But this is run a close second by Professor Basil Hennessy's observation:

Perhaps the most relevant item of von Däniken's evidence is on page 42. There has not, to the author's knowledge, been any shred of evidence to suggest that coprolites (fossil dung) found in a pit at the proto-neolithic site of Tepe Asiab were anything other than human; but if another origin is sought, to be consistent with von Däniken's other archaeological claims it could only be Bovine.

How do von Däniken and those like him—for he is not, alas, unique—not only get away with this sort of thing but indeed make vast fortunes out of it? Here is one suggestion, offered by Gordon Whitaker, the Lecturer in Aztec Studies at Brandeis University, Massachusetts:

It's very easy when reading *Chariots of the Gods?* and its sequel, *Return to the Stars*, to be led to the conclusion that our Big Brothers in Outer Space had a special affection for the lands of the Western Hemisphere, since von Däniken's works abound in references to the marvels of civilization they left behind there—far too advanced for mere Earthlings to have created.

Von Däniken takes advantage of the fact that the history of the civilizations in that hemisphere are neither common knowledge nor taught in high school in even the barest of outlines. Because of this lack he is able to distort the facts in any way he wishes, free from the fear that the general public, including students, will have the knowledge to see through his claims.

Which is fair enough as far as it goes, but it only hints at the scope of the problem. The knowledge exists to refute writers like von Däniken. Often, moreover, the necessary data are absolutely non-specialised; you don't require training or education to comprehend a statement like the following, for example:

'The man who writes under the name of Lobsang Rampa was born Cyril Hoskins in Plympton, Devon, and trained not as a lama but as a plumber. On his own admission he has only been a "Tibetan" personality since the day when he fell out of a tree in June 1949 and hit his head.' (Paraphrasing Dr Christopher Evans in *Cults of Unreason*, Panther, 1974.)

I very distinctly recall hearing a BBC radio broadcast, one of a series on great hoaxes, in which Rampa's publisher confessed to the way in which he had been hoodwinked. (*The Imposters 3*: 'The Tibetan Lama' broadcast 15 May 1962.)

Ask yourself how many copies *The Third Eye* would be selling today were it a legal requirement to put the above statement on the cover.

Perhaps the single most wholly dishonest book I have ever had the misfortune to set eyes on is the one by Louis Pauwels and Jacques Bergier known variously as *The Dawn of Magic* and *The Morning of the Magicians*.

I grant it that dubious distinction because in most cases— not being myself grounded in science—I have to refer to others in order to refute with borrowed authority what I suspect (all too often correctly) of being rubbish.

In this particular case I was able to rely on my own reference library and a couple of helpful friends. I would not for a second maintain that I've spotted all the falsehoods. But I have certainly spotted sufficient to embark on an undertaking that I will derive great satisfaction from: an extensive hatchet-job.

Not, of course, that it will do much good . . . but it will be balm for my soul, even though I am obliged to be selective; a full-scale counterblast would require another volume as large as the original.

Here is a passage which refers to an alchemist who is said to have written, under the name Fulcanelli, a couple of books on his subject 'about the year 1920'. Bergier is of course one of the co-authors of *The Dawn of Magic*.

Please note the date, and the statement: 'The following is an exact account of the conversation . . .'

One afternoon in June 1937, Jacques Bergier thought there was good reason to believe that he was in the presence of Fulcanelli.

It was at the request of André Helbronner that my friend met this mysterious personage in the prosaic surroundings of a test laboratory at the offices of the Gas Board in Paris. The following is an exact account of the conversation that then took place:

'M. André Helbronner, whose assistant I believe you are, is carrying out research on nuclear energy. M. Helbronner has been good enough to keep me informed as to the results of some of his experiments, notably the appearance of radio-activity corresponding to plutonium when a bismuth rod is volatilized by an electric discharge in deuterium at high pressure. You are on the brink of success, as indeed are several other of our scientists today. May I be allowed to warn you to be careful? The research in which you and your colleagues are engaged is fraught with terrible dangers, not only for yourselves, but for the whole human race.'

(*The Dawn of Magic*, Panther, 1964, p. 77)

And so on.

Did you notice what kind of trick Pauwels and Bergier are attempting to put over on their readers? If not, recall the date given (June 1937) and consider the following:

PLUTONIUM, a silvery-white, radioactive metallic element; symbol Pu; at. no. 94; at. wt. 242; sp. gr. 19.8; m.p. 639°C.; b.p. 3,235°C. A TRANSURANIUM ELEMENT in the actinide series of the PERIODIC TABLE, plutonium is very electropositive, quite reactive chemically, gives off warmth by reason of alpha-particle emission, and very large pieces can cause sufficient heat to make water boil. Upon oxidation, it turns yellow. Small amounts of plutonium occur in uranium ores, and it is produced artificially by bombarding uranium with neutrons. It was first discovered in 1940 in the cyclotron at Berkeley, Calif., by Seaborg, McMillan, Kennedy, and Wahl. (*The Cadillac Modern Encyclopedia*, 1973)

A few lines lower on the page, the alleged alchemist—

then picked up Frederick Soddy's *The Interpretation of Radium* and read as follows: 'I believe that there have been civilizations in the past that were familiar with atomic energy, and that by misusing it they were totally destroyed.'

Now this is heady stuff. Soddy is a man worth quoting; not only was he one of the pioneering researchers into radioactivity, but he coined a word known now to almost everybody —he invented the term 'isotope'.

It would have been even more worth quoting him if he had actually said that. Smelling some sort of rat, because the phraseology struck me as anachronistic, I requested the librarian at the Science Museum to trace the actual statement, which he did within a remarkably short time. Now contrast the version given by Pauwels and Bergier with the original:

Was then this old association of the power of transmutation
with the elixir of life merely a coincidence? I prefer to
believe it may be an echo from one of many previous epochs
in the unrecorded history of the world, of an age of men
which have trod before the road we are treading to-day, in a
past possibly so remote that even the very atoms of its
civilisation literally have had time to disintegrate. (Frederick
Soddy: *The Interpretation of Radium*, John Murray, 1909)

I'd have thought that that was a useful enough quotation in
its own right, particularly since a page or two later we find
Soddy speculating as to whether the legend of the Fall of Man
might be interpreted in terms of the collapse of a civilisation
more advanced than our own. But it must, I feel, be admitted
that the difference between the original and what is attributed
to Soddy in *The Dawn of Magic* cannot be ascribed to translation
and re-translation.

Incidentally, he made those remarks during 'a series of six
free popular experimental lectures' in 1908. Radioactivity was
new—and news—in those days, and the discovery that one
element could transmute into another by radioactive decay
had opened for the first time (in the West, at least) the debate
which endures into our own day about continuous creation . . .
the subject, indeed, which led Soddy to pass his comment about
the Fall. One had to be cautious about such matters for fear of
fundamentalists, of course.

Another quotation from *The Dawn of Magic*, which calls to
mind Haldane's acerb comment about the likelihood that a new
religion would enshrine what passed for modern thought in the
previous generation:

All our knowledge of the atom and its nucleus is based on the
'Saturnian' model of Nagasoka and Rutherford: the nucleus
and its belt, or ring, of electrons.   (p. 86)

And, a few pages later:

The old alchemic texts affirm that the keys to the secrets of matter are to be found in Saturn. By a strange coincidence, everything we know today in nuclear physics is based on a definition of the 'Saturnian' atom. (p. 89)

A while ago I made reference to people whose knowledge of 'physics' appears to derive from Jarry. What passes for scientific information in the case of these two (or passed, at the time they wrote the book—one tries to be fair) is fractionally more recent, and no more correct or reliable for that. Half a truth, it seems, is better to grow bread.

Perhaps the previous complaint was too rarefied for some people. On the same page, however, can be found in the form of a footnote this remarkable passage:

Professor Ralph Milne Farley, United States Senator and Professor of Modern Physics at the West Point Military Academy, has drawn attention to the fact that some biologists think that old age is due to the accumulation of heavy water in the organism. The alchemists' elixir of life might then be a substance that eliminates selectively heavy water. Such substances exist in evaporated water. Why, then, should they not be found in liquid water when treated in a certain way? But could so important a discovery be published without danger? Mr. Farley imagines a secret society of immortals, or quasi-immortals, who have existed for centuries and reproduce themselves by co-option. Such a society, keeping aloof from politics and the affairs of men, would have every chance of remaining undetected . . . (p. 86)

Now on the face of it that looks like a straightforward and authoritative statement. There are references to the kind of data which one may track down in the public library if not in one's own home: 'United States Senator'—'Professor of Modern Physics at West Point'—and suchlike. There is an almost incantatory quality which lulls suspicion.

No such person as Ralph Milne Farley exists. No such person as Ralph Milne Farley ever has existed. It is possible that there may be, or may have been, a person bearing that name; if so, however, he was never a US Senator nor was he a professor at West Point.

How can I be so categorical? Because 'Ralph Milne Farley' was the pen-name of a guy called Roger Sherman Hoar, and the statements which Pauwels and Bergier dressed up to give the impression of factuality . . . constitute a bad summary of the plot of a novel called *The Immortals*, serialised in six parts in the American magazine *Argosy* beginning on 17 November 1934. At which time, incidentally, I myself was just under two months old. How did I cotton on to this particular lie? When I was twelve or thirteen I bought a shilling paperback edition of the book; science fiction was scarce in Britain in those days, and one had to snap up whatever appeared. And because SF was so rare one tended to recall with great vividness and clarity what little material did come to hand.

Earlier in this talk I said that at least we SF people have the decency to remind our audience, when it seems necessary, that what we are trading in *is* fiction. Contrast that attitude with the one adhered to by Pauwels and Bergier, which indeed they blatantly admit:

> Like Fred Hoyle, and many other British scientists, Eric Temple Bell writes fantastic stories and essays (under the pseudonym of John Taine). Only the most naïve reader would imagine that these merely represent a relaxation for great minds. It is the only way to disseminate certain truths that are inacceptable to official philosophy. (p. 257)

What in heaven's name are we to do when we find that our fiction is being palmed off under the guise of fact?

I have been complimented by our French science-fiction friends to the extent of being invited as guest of honour at their first national SF convention. I invariably enjoy my visits to that country. I've made many good friends across the Channel, and I have met many talented writers—indeed, I've translated some French SF into English and hope to translate more.

But one thing does mar my contacts with French SF people, and occasionally makes me very gloomy. When I'm asked about such books as *The Dawn of Magic* and *Chariots of the Gods?*, and not only say what I think but document my reasons, I find many of them shying away, closing their minds to argument. It's their belief that *all* SF writers should care as little for 'dull and boring' fact as do their idols: von Däniken, Pauwels, Bergier, Kast, Velikovsky, Fort . . .

Forgive that divagation. Here's another quote from *The Dawn of Magic*:

> Savages suffering from infectious illnesses eat *penicillium notatum* (a kind of mushroom): this must be a form of imitative magic whereby they seek to increase their vigour by consuming this phallic symbol. (p. 106)

To which all one can honestly say is that if *that* is the form taken by the respective phalluses of Messrs Pauwels and Bergier, they are missing the chance to make a major contribution to the study of human anatomy. *Penicillium notatum*—in case you didn't know?—is a mould.

(At this point one has reached page 106 of my copy of the book, out of a total of 304 pages . . .)

Ah, yes. Now we come to a pair of quotations which have always seemed to indicate to me that even the authors found their effusions so revolting they could not endure to re-read what they had already written. (Would that this had been the case with their over-credulous followers . . .)

This appears on page 112 of my copy:

> When the War in Europe ended on 8th May, 1945, missions of investigation were immediately sent out to visit Germany after her defeat. Their reports have been published; the catalogue alone has 300 pages. Germany had only been separated from the rest of the world since 1933. In twelve years the technical evolution of the Reich developed along strangely divergent lines. Although the Germans were behindhand as regards the atomic bomb, they had perfected giant rockets unmatched by any in America or Russia. They may not have had radar, but they had perfected a system of infra-red ray detectors which were quite as effective.

You will note that that refers to May 1945. And it states that the Germans 'may not have had radar'.

Watch the birdie! This appears on page 185:

We are in April 1942. Germany is putting her whole strength into the war. Nothing, it would seem, could distract the technicians, scientists and military chiefs from the performance of their immediate tasks.

Nevertheless, an expedition organized with the approval of Goering, Himmler and Hitler set out from the Reich surrounded by the greatest secrecy. The members of this expedition were some of the greatest experts on radar. Under the direction of Dr. Heinz Fisher, well known for his work on infra-red rays, they disembarked on the island of Rügen in the Baltic. The expedition was equipped with the most up-to-date radar apparatus, despite the fact that these instruments were still rare at that time, and distributed over the principal nerve-centres of the German defence system.

However, the observations to be carried out on the island of Rügen were considered by the Admiralty General Staff as of capital importance for the offensive which Hitler was preparing to launch on every front.

Immediately on arrival at their destination Dr. Fisher aimed his radar at the sky at an angle of 45 degrees.

And so on . . . Bear in mind both quotations are from one book, and that of course Germany was *not* isolated for twelve years.

And in the same book again:

Genesis does not mention giants, but this omission is abundantly atoned for in Jewish and Moslem traditions. (p. 162)

You don't say! Well, I hope you don't . . . This is *Genesis* chapter VI verse 4:

There were giants in the earth in those days; and also after that, when the sons of God came in unto the daughters of men, and they bare *children* to them, the same *became* mighty men which *were* of old, men of renown.

It would appear that not only do Pauwels and Bergier omit to re-read their own writings; they also omit to read their source-material. It's not as though *Genesis* chapter VI were a long way from the beginning of the Bible . . .

In the company of Pauwels and Bergier one makes the acquaintance of some truly remarkable scientific investigators. My favourite is Zimanski.

> Zimanski, the German scientist from Tubingen and a pupil of the brilliant Conrad Lorenz, spent three years studying snails, becoming so familiar with their language and behaviour that they actually looked upon him as one of themselves. (p. 217)

Which in the mating season must have posed certain problems, snails being hermaphroditic . . .

What is the attraction in this kind of sloppy nonsense? Myself, I have always found fact infinitely more interesting than myths and falsehoods; indeed, I gave Chad Mulligan in *Stand On Zanzibar* a comment that precisely corresponds to my own feelings—that the real universe has a marvellous and unique quality, inasmuch as it and only it can take us completely by surprise. (Can it be that some people are frightened by that attribute?)

At all events there is a positive epidemic of mental myopia today. Among the books I intended to read prior to delivering this address was Lyall Watson's *Supernature*. Unfortunately, even before I reached the start of Part One, I ran across the following improbable remark:

> . . . despite the fact that she was once caught cheating very clumsily at a public performance, Kuleshova also possesses a talent that cannot reasonably be shrugged off . . . (Book Club Associates edition, 1974)

Now I may be unduly cynical, but the first thing brought to my mind by the statement that Kuleshova (a Russian woman who claimed to be able to distinguish colours, etc., without using normal eyesight) was once caught cheating clumsily at a public performance, is the corollary that on other occasions her cheating was not clumsy.

I have, I may say, precisely the same opinion in respect of Uri Geller. Why is it that hard-headed, practical scientists can be selectively blind in areas where, even though they themselves are not experts, experts do exist and can be easily consulted? I often wish that Harry Houdini were still among us. It would do Geller's dupes a power of good to study his exposure of Argamasilla, 'The Spaniard with X-ray Eyes':

> As credentials, this young man brought letters purporting to have been written by the Nobel prize winner, Prof. Richet, and from Prof. Geley; likewise, from noted scientists of Spain who attested the fact that Argamasilla, unqualifiedly, came through all tests and that he had proved conclusively to their satisfaction *that he could read through metal.* (*Houdini on Magic,* Dover, 1953)

To their satisfaction, perhaps. Not to Houdini's. His meticulous analysis of the trickery employed is a model of its kind, and a warning certain persons would do well to take to heart. This was his considered view of 'psychic' powers:

> When I started to investigate Spiritualism more than twenty-five years ago, I did so with an open mind and a sincere desire to learn if truth was involved in Spiritualism. During all those years, more than a quarter of a century, and up to the present moment, I have not received any convincing evidence, and of all the mediums I have encountered, not one of them has satisfied me with the genuineness of psychical phenomena. To the contrary, I have never failed to detect a fraud, or at least a possible solution on a perfectly rational basis. (*ibid.*)

Even in the case of the Spaniard whose genuineness was attested by a Nobel prize-winner . . .

All too often people become willing accomplices in their own duping, discounting or ignoring evidence to the contrary of what it suits their taste to believe. There are of course situations in which they have no alternative but to be duped—for instance, by advertising, which sometimes makes claims that the person in the street could not possibly verify or disprove.

And above all government uses deceit to maintain power. One does not need the total control over the media exercised by the Nazis in order to make the public believe falsehoods; however, it is naturally much more efficient if you're operating a dictatorship. For many years I declined to go to Spain on holiday, not wishing to subsidise a Fascist régime. Then we made the acquaintance of a young Catalan who said that on the contrary we must go to Spain; had it not been for meeting visitors from abroad, so complete was Franco's hold on the educational system he might—he said—never have realised that life was different and better in other countries.

Examples of total indoctrination on even grander scales than that abound in SF. Best-known of all, doubtless, is the job held by Winston Smith in *1984*, rewriting not just history but the most recent newspapers so as to make the record match the requirements of the moment.

Here's another, a particularly ingenious one drawn from the work of a science fiction writer whom I greatly admire: Philip K. Dick. In *The Penultimate Truth* propaganda experts are revising history completely in order to remove the stigma of Nazism from Germany. Thus during World War II Hitler is to be shown flying to America for consultations with Roosevelt. Here's the protagonist, Joseph Adams, putting his finger on a fatal flaw in a key 'documentary' designed to underpin the new version of events:

Adams said harshly, "It's in the arrival of Hitler at the 'secret US Air Force base near Washington, DC,' that the technical error occurs, and it's incredible that no one's noticed it. First of all, in World War Two there was no US Air Force."

She stared at him.

"It was still called the Army Air Corps," Adams said. "Not yet a separate branch of the military. But that's nothing; that could be a minor error in the aud commentary—a mere nothing. Look." He swiftly removed the spool from the scanner, picked up the spool of version B; eyes to the scanner he deftly ran the spool, on and on, until he arrived at the scene, in episode sixteen, that he wanted; he then sat back and motioned her to follow the scene.

For a time Colleen was silent as she watched. "Here comes his jet now," she murmured. "In for the landing, late at night, at the—yes, you're right; the commentator is calling it a 'US Air Force base,' and I dimly recall—"

"His *jet*," Adams grated.

Halting the spool, Colleen looked up at him.

"Hitler lands secretly in the US in May of 1942," Adams said, "in a Boeing 707 fan-jet. Those didn't come into use until the mid-1960s. There was only one jet plane extant during World War Two, a German-made fighter, and it never saw service."

"Oh my god," Colleen said, open-mouthed.

"But it worked," Adams said. "People in Pac-Peop believed it—by 1982 they were so used to seeing jets that they forgot that in '42 there were only what they called—" He couldn't remember.

"Prop planes," Colleen said.

And now . . .

Earlier on, I mentioned that data exist to refute people like von Däniken. What I did not stress was the difficulty of getting hold of them. Let me turn around almost everything I've been saying and look at it from a totally contrasting angle.

In that passage by Philip Dick which I just quoted, the protagonist is made to say that there was only one jet plane extant during World War II, a German-made fighter, and it never saw service.

When I read that I started to frown. What about the Gloster-Whittle? What about the Meteor? What about the De Haviland Vampire? And wasn't there at least one Italian jet astonishingly early?

So I consulted the handiest available reference-book: *Flying Machines* by Roy MacGregor-Hastie (N.E.L., 1965). From it I learned that Phil was partly right and so was I:

The Heinkel 'He 178' first flew in 1939, then the Italian

'Caproni-Campini' in the next year. Seeing the enemy busy and successful in this field, the British War Cabinet gave Frank Whittle its overdue support for his programme, and Whittle had the Gloster 'E28/39' in the air by May 1941. The Gloster 'Meteor' went into service in 1943, and achieved a top speed of 480 mph. Yet, because of the delays in backing Whittle, his German rivals managed to make much more progress by the end of the war. The twin-jet Messerschmitt 'ME 262', which first flew in 1942, had already a top speed of 525 mph and according to Gibbs-Smith was 'the world's first operational jet-propelled combat aeroplane'.

And captious people like me may recall that during World War II there was a US Army Air Force, not Air Corps. Never mind, though. Dick was writing a novel, not a textbook.

But . . . how reliable is that authoritative-seeming work, *Flying Machines*? Turn back only two pages, and you will find this highly improbable assertion:

The Second World War, in which air power was decisive, favoured a development of aviation both unprecedented and dramatic. The 1939 speed (469·142 mph, Messerschmitt 'Bf 109R'), altitude (56·046 Italy, 1938) and distance (7·58 miles, Vickers Wellesley) records were soon to be almost 'historic'.

Yes indeed. Not only does the book inform us that the world's long-distance flying record in 1939 was roughly equal to the distance from Hampstead to Camberwell; it also declares that the altitude record was 56·046 but neglects to tell us fifty-six of *what*.

And this, I'm afraid, is only the start.

You'll remember that in order to refute claims by von Däniken about the tombs in the Valley of the Kings I quoted the opinions of a distinguished Semitic scholar, E. C. B. Mac-Laurin. In passing, in the passage I cited, he said: 'quite irreconcilably, he [von Däniken] states that the remains of an electric battery was found in Mesopotamia'.

From the context and the choice of words it seems plain that

Mr MacLaurin does not believe the remains of an electric battery to have been found in Mesopotamia. In a certain respect this is correct. Not one battery, but a considerable number of them have been dug up, and it is now some years since *New Scientist*, a journal of impeccable credentials, devoted a long article to them. It appears that a small group of metal-workers stumbled on the principle of electroplating, and not unexpectedly acquired a reputation as wizards and sorcerers in consequence. (cf. *The Ancient Engineers*, L. Sprague de Camp, Ballantine, 1974, p. 252.)

Sheer ignorance is not the weakness of von Däniken alone . . .

Here's an example of another kind of problem all too frequently encountered. Let's turn back to *The Dawn of Magic*.

An ancient method of hardening steel practised in the Near East was to plunge a red-hot blade into the body of a prisoner. This is a typical act of magic: the object being to transfer the adversary's warlike qualities to the sword. The practice was known to the Crusaders in the West, who had noticed that Damascus steel was in fact harder than European steel. As an experiment, steel was dipped into water in which animal skins had been immersed. The same result was obtained. In the nineteenth century it was discovered that these results were due to the presence of organic nitrogen. In the twentieth century, when the problem of liquefying gases had been solved, the method was perfected by immersing steel in liquid nitrogen at a low temperature. In this form nitration has been adopted in our technology.   (pp. 41–42)

That passage caught my eye for a particular reason. I'd run across a similar explanation for the origin of Damascus steel many years previously, which differed only in minor details— for instance, that the discovery was made when some caliph or other wanted to inflict a peculiarly horrible punishment on his worst enemy and decreed that a red-hot sword be plunged into his body. (Indeed I retailed the story in one of my early books, *No Future In It*.)

But I'd always been under the impression that it was the presence of carbon in the quenching-solution that made the steel so tough. I know virtually nothing about metallurgy, and

I do try, so far as is humanly possible, to establish the facts before discussing any subject; I hope to learn even from people whom—to be candid—I despise. I think finding out is fun!

So, being unacquainted with the term 'nitration' (though able to guess at its approximate meaning, of course) I turned, logically enough, to Chatto's *Modern Science Dictionary*. This is what I found:

> **nitration.** (1) The introduction of a nitro group, NO_2, into an organic compound; (2) the last stage of nitrification.

Plainly the former definition was not relevant; however, the latter seemed promising, so I looked in the next column expecting to find an entry for nitrification.

There wasn't one.

'Oh, what a dusty answer gets the soul . . . !'

I don't mean I was unable to track down a definition. Just that I had to consult a regular dictionary instead of a science dictionary. And I remain no wiser about the respective importance of nitrogen as against carbon in the production of Damascus steel.

Still on the subject of *The Dawn of Magic*: remember that I looked up the entry on plutonium in an encyclopaedia—*The Cadillac Modern Encyclopedia*, to be precise—and discovered that it was neither known nor named in 1937, having first been identified in 1940?

Splendid. But that same work of reference will straightfacedly inform you that in a mile there are not as many feet as there are yards: 1580 against 1760.

No, I am *not* joking. It's there in black and white, under the head 'English System' on page 511.

With a mixture of incredulity and horror I have been documenting, over the past few years, the way in which pure nonsense has been acquiring the status of authoritative fact—and I do not mean solely in the context of fakery and charlatanism. *The Oxford Dictionary of English Etymology*, for example, will unblushingly assure you that oxygen is 'the most abundant of the elements'. Really? Then what about this?

. . . the chemical constitution of the universe is surprisingly uniform. It

was found that about 55 per cent of cosmic matter is hydrogen and about 44 per cent helium; the remaining 1 per cent accounts for all heavier elements.

But of course that's only the opinion of George Gamow, in *The Creation of the Universe* (Mentor, 1957).

Likewise, my copy of the Penguin *Roget* maintains that in nuclear physics there is a particle called a 'mucon', and what is more there is another called a 'hyperion' . . . though fortunately no attempt is made to compare it with a satyr.

For heaven's sake! If our most distinguished lexicographers are only semi-literate in science, how can we expect the casual purchaser of a book by Velikovsky or von Däniken to know any better? Even someone who grows suspicious and tries to confirm or disprove the wilder statements made by these hoaxers runs the risk of finding that other authorities are questionable, inaccurate and sometimes downright wrong. It is often stated that because of a misplaced decimal-point one work of reference after another, over a period of many years, gave a molecular weight for haemoglobin which was ten times too large. Not until a researcher realised that this could not be reconciled with his results was the error detected. I have neither chapter nor verse for this particular story; my own experience, however, inclines me to believe it.

The chief grounds I have for being afraid of the current wave of antiscientism in Western society derive from recent historical events. Above all, the Nazis not only believed in 'pure races' of humans and the mystic power of 'blood'; they adopted Hans Hörbiger's *Welteislehre* so enthusiastically that according to Martin Gardner the Propaganda Ministry had to issue a directive explaining 'one can be a good National Socialist without believing in the WEL'. (*Fads and Fallacies in the Name of Science*, Dover, 1957)

You may not be familiar with this doctrine; it obliged one to accept, *inter alia*, that the Milky Way is a ring of gigantic blocks of ice and that the Moon is covered in ice 140 miles thick.

Laughable? At the time . . . no. Consider these quotations from the cult's literature which were cited by Willy Ley of much-lamented memory, the rocket engineer who fled the Nazis:

"Our Nordic ancestors grew strong in ice and snow; belief in the World Ice is consequently the natural heritage of Nordic Man."

"Just as it needed a child of Austrian culture—Hitler!—to put the Jewish politicians in their place, so it needed an Austrian to cleanse the world of Jewish science."

"The Führer, by his very life, has proved how much a so-called 'amateur' can be superior to self-styled professionals; it needed another 'amateur' to give us complete understanding of the universe." (Gardner, *loc. cit.*)

Confronted with echoes from the past like those, one looks with a new and perhaps more worried eye at such remarks as that with which Ved Mehta climaxed a discussion of possible revolution in India in the article following the one I quoted earlier:

For the first time there is talk here of military dictatorship.

To a great extent this disastrous state of affairs can be ascribed—one is obliged to insist on the fact—to unwarranted arrogance on the part of those who, whether consciously or unconsciously, regard themselves as having inherited the rôle of ancient priests, who behave like a whole covey of Melchizedeks. Of them all (and they are numerous) the worst offenders seem to have congregated at the interface where most of us have our only real contact with 'science'; in other words they are in the medical profession. The psychological impact on the lay public of X-ray machines, electrocardiographs, anaesthetic machines and endless shelves of pills and potions, is incomparably closer —particularly since matters of life and death are involved—to the popular idea of science than what is found in school science laboratories. Being drilled through experiments, so-called, and marked down if your result does not agree with what appears at the back of the teacher's textbook, has little or nothing to do with real science!

Here is an example from our grandparents' day of the damage that can be done by an obsessive in a position of influence—and who is to say whether it is more or less harmful than the damage due to the von Dänikens and the Velikovskys? This is Alex Comfort, in *The Anxiety Makers*, discussing William Arbuthnot Lane, the dedicated apostle of liquid paraffin who believed that 'intestinal stasis'—i.e. constipation— was the cause of duodenal ulcers, appendicitis, cancer, tuberculosis, rheumatoid arthritis and degeneration of the species, at the very least, and consequently devised an operation to remove the entire colon.

> Before this, Guy's had used little liquid paraffin, and that chiefly for external purposes. Soon it was arriving in drums, like beer at an inn. The fate of the ingested paraffin began to be appreciated when, years later, Lane's patients and disciples began to die of natural causes, and mineral oil could be squeezed from their livers at post-mortem like water from so many sponges. Flavoured emulsion, with or without the violent and repetitive purgative phenolphthalein, appeared on the market for popular consumption. In the Second World War, it was banned as an ingredient of salad dressing because of the risk of tissue storage. The wheel had come full pharmacological circle.
>
> Lane never had his own colon out (there were very few other surgeons who could have performed the operation with his consummate technical skill), but in his declining years he consumed increasing quantities of liquid paraffin, and the resulting leakage made him an unwelcome guest. (*The Anxiety Makers*, Panther, 1968)

Lane died in 1938. That the attitude he epitomised (mitigated in his case, as Comfort makes clear, by many constructive projects to improve diet and encourage better sanitation) is not dead, can be illustrated by this excerpt from a recent issue of *New Scientist*. The author is director of the Massachusetts drug rehabilitation agency.

> Professionals further mystify the public by becoming seduced into thinking that the more esoteric and technological their

vocabulary and machinery, the more professional they are. American medicine, for example, has come to feel that it is truest to its purposes amid the marvels of transplant surgery when a much less fancy devotion to basic public health would alleviate considerably more suffering and prolong considerably more lives. In fact, it is possible that the lust for aggressive therapy by our physicians comes close to being a public health menace itself. (23 January 1975)

Small wonder, is it not, that when someone comes along with an impressive vocabulary and a pile of 'facts' and addresses him- or herself direct to the public over the heads of the specialists and the professionals, a huge audience expresses its collective gratitude by shelling out for millions of copies of worthless books? Indeed, after struggling with some recent articles even in publications like *New Scientist* intended to help the layman keep in touch, it's a positive relief to turn to a down-to-earth, matter-of-fact work like David Conway's *Magic, an Occult Primer*, and discover such commonsensical observations as his statement that 'even magicians have their off days' . . .

One is hard put to it to decide whether arrogance is a besetting sin among us or a—less grandiose—defence mechanism. Personally I suspect the latter. How often do we recall the briefness of the span during which scientific method has enjoyed the ascendancy in even our allegedly 'advanced' society? How often do we think back over the 'received wisdom' of our childhood, now abandoned? (I've been taught three entirely distinct ways of dressing a burn since I was first old enough not to drown out the advice with screams of pain. Each in its day was 'the last word', of course.) How often do we reflect on Disraeli who took the side of the angels, and remind ourselves that those who pretended for centuries—even millennia—to absolute knowledge found their customary and long-secure redoubts overwhelmed within a matter of a few short generations, leaving them with scarcely a figleaf to cover their intellectual nakedness?

And how often do we try and picture the same fate overtaking us?

Well . . . if we happen to be into science fiction, pretty frequently!

This, surely, is the *raison d'être* of science fiction, inasmuch as it possesses one over and above the simple business of entertainment. At its best, SF is the medium in which our miserable certainty that tomorrow will be different from today in ways we can't predict, can be transmuted to a sense of excitement and anticipation, occasionally evolving into awe. Poised between intransigent scepticism and uncritical credulity, it is *par excellence* the literature of the open mind. Here to end on is a quotation from—again—J. B. S. Haldane, a man with far greater insight into his own motivation and a far greater capacity for elucidating it to others than I can boast of. With this passage I, and I believe a great many of my colleagues, would wish to be associated:

Our only hope of understanding the universe is to look at it from as many different points of view as possible. This is one of the reasons why the data of the mystical consciousness can usefully supplement those of the mind in its normal state. Now, my own suspicion is that the universe is not only queerer than we suppose, but queerer than we *can* suppose. I have read and heard many attempts at a systematic account of it, from materialism and theosophy to the Christian system or that of Kant, and I have always felt that they were much too simple. I suspect that there are more things in heaven and earth than are dreamed of, or can be dreamed of, in any philosophy. That is the reason why I have no philosophy myself, and must be my excuse for dreaming. (Haldane, *op. cit.*)

I offer you the same excuse for writing science fiction . . . but no apology.

5

Worlds Beside Worlds

HARRY HARRISON

HARRY HARRISON

Harry Harrison spoke without notes, prowling up and down the stage, threatening interjectors with instant retribution. He allowed himself to be sidetracked a number of times, and it was in the course of his asides that the audience probably caught the flavour, more clearly than from any other speaker, of what life is like for the science fiction professional: funny stories about agents, tragic stories about what Hollywood did with *Make Room! Make Room!* when they filmed it. Through it all, his fierce loyalty to the genre which, he is the first to admit, is often shabby and second rate, shone through. He has a clear-sighted view of the literature he loves, its failings as well as its strengths.

There is no way in which we could print Harry's speech as it was delivered—it was as much a happening as a lecture. However, there was a perfectly coherent line of development, and he very decently wrote it out for me afterwards (shorn, in some ways sadly, of all its baroque and entertaining if irrelevant verbal adornments).

I have said previously that each of the lectures was not to be just about science fiction. Each lecture was to be about 'science fiction *and*'. In this case the conjunction will be surprising to all those who think of science fiction as exclusively concerned with the future, not the present, let alone the past—it is 'science fiction and history'. (Looked at the other way around, history itself is concerned with the greatest of all science fiction themes —evolution and change.)

The great game in science fiction is titled *What If*, and it is perhaps one of the things that topples a mainstream novel over into the SF category. *What if* we have an atomic war classifies Shute's *On The Beach* as science fiction, while *what if* certain nasty political things happen brings *1984* and *When the Kissing Had to Stop* into the same category. This process even works in time past so that many of the *what if* the French invade Britain novels, such as *The Battle of Dorking* are considered ur-SF by the critical aggrandisers.

All of these themes have one factor in common—extension into the future at the time of writing. When the *what if* game is played in the past it assumes entirely new dimensions. And is entirely separate from, though it can be related to, the *What If There Is Time Travel* game. Wells first played this one with his time machine that travelled forward in time to give us glimpses of a fixed future, dips into the constantly rushing, always unchangeable, river of time. Other time trips to the future followed, such as Wright's *The World Below*, and the variation of alternate possible futures considered in Williamson's *The Legion of Time* in 1938.

In *The Legion of Time* there appears, for the first time in a novel-length magazine serial, a concept different from the river of time theory. *What if* time is more like an ever-branching tree with countless possible futures? If each decision we make affects the future then there must be an infinite number of futures. In the river-of-time concept the future is immutable. If, on the way to work in the morning, we decide to take the bus instead of the tube and are killed in a bus accident, then that death was pre-destined. But if time is ever-branching then there are two futures—one in which we die in the accident and another where we live on, having taken the tube.[1] It therefore follows

[1] There is a strong whiff here of the ancient theological wrangle about free-will and predestination. After the countless books and discussions on

consistently, or at least consistently to a science fiction author's mind, that if there are an infinite set of futures why there must then be an infinite set of pasts as well. And, if this be true, then a time traveller can go back to alter the past and thereby alter the present. Or a present. Or a hideously large number of presents. Or is there such a thing as a single 'present' if this theory is to be considered?

All of this led to a great number of SF stories located in the misty borderland between time travel and multiple time tracks. Paradoxes abounded; what happens if you kill your grandfather?—and interesting permutations such as Heinlein's "All You Zombies" where every single character, male, female and joint offspring, is the same character. (This theme is examined differently by the same author in "By His Bootstraps".)

Out of all this evolved the concept of the parallel-world theme. As in all of science fiction there are no hard and fast rules. Whenever someone attempts to draw up rules or definitions someone else instantly breaks them. In the roughest way then, the theme of parallel worlds can be broken down into two main categories and one sub-category. They are:

A. The parallel worlds in the present.
B. The parallel world in the present.
    (b) Changing this world in the past to alter the present.

A. is the far simpler one to handle and much used in the pulps of the 'forties and 'fifties. In this there are an infinite number of parallel worlds, all brought about by differing events in the past. They are infinitely close yet infinitely distant, since each has its distinct 'vibration energy' or other meaningless term that keeps them apart. Enter machine that permits motion sideways in

<hr />

this topic I feel the entire controversy was laid to rest by Norman Spinrad in the October 1974 *Analog* in an article entitled "Psychesomics: The Emerging Science of Consciousness". Here, after explaining all of the current facts and theories regarding human consciousness, and showing that no possible pattern of human consciousness could ever be repeated for even a microsecond, Spinrad adds, in a most offhand manner, a a throwaway sentence. 'So much for determinism.' So much indeed! Again, as always in the past, what appears to be a serious theological dispute turns out to be angels on a pinhead yet one more time.

time to other parallel worlds, enter nifty action plots as well. Neither the past nor the future is relevant to these stories since motion between them is always in the present.

B. is the more complex and the more fun to both write and read. If B.(b) does not enter into the plot directly there is always an awareness of it which is why I do not classify it as a separate category. These are the *What If* stories where a change was made in the past to give us a different present. *What if* the South had won the American Civil War? Moore's *Bring the Jubilee* is the answer to that one. *What if* the Germans and Japanese had won World War II? Dick's *Man in the High Castle* mulls this one over.

Both of these books depend upon a change in military history, this being the simplest and easiest way to bring about radical changes in society. But, as in the new history, we have new considerations in science fiction. Culture and philosophy can be as interesting and vital as a list of battles won and lost. Religion is of course the great divider, as we see in Aldiss's "Danger: Religion!" I dipped a toe into theological waters myself in a story titled "The Wicked Flee". What I wanted was a world where the Catholic church ran everything. I got this by the simple—and simple-minded—device of killing both Martin Luther and Henry VIII in their youth. (Ignoring, for the sake of the story, the historical thrusts that permitted the acceptance of their changes.)

Plotting a parallel-world story must, of necessity, rest upon one of two choices. The author can make his change in the past, then speculate upon what changes this might bring about. (A volcanic eruption blows up all Europe in the early fifteenth century. Modern civilisation must therefore come from the East and not the West.) Or the author may want to set a story in some exotic present—so how must he alter the past to bring this about? (The world is populated by pig-like humanoids. At the precisely worked out moment in the past a pig eats the first intelligent hominid offspring.)

These slightly exotic examples reveal that the parallel-world theme can be a remarkably satisfying and rewarding area of speculation. It has to be played to very exacting rules and no cheating can be allowed. It is very much like a chess game. Before the first chess piece is moved there must be an infinite number of ways that the game can be played. Yet with the simple move of KP to K4 the future possibilities are halved. And so on with each move.

I can demonstrate the concept far better than I can explain it. If, in doing so, I can give some insight into the warped synapses of the science fiction writer's mind we can consider this as a fringe benefit. The book under discussion is titled *A Transatlantic Tunnel, Hurrah!*

Genesis. I do not remember quite what circumstances raised the question, but I do remember the question quite clearly. Would it be possible to build a transatlantic tunnel? Technically, I imagined it would be. Modern technology and materials would surely enable construction of a tunnel at continental shelf depths. As to abyssal depths—why the SF invention of the Stronger Material should take care of that if the question did arise. Physically it could be built. I suppose in the '30s the speculation would have ended there and the story would have been written in a burst of hunger-driven energy and flogged instantly to *Incredibly Awful Adventures* for a quarter of a cent a word, and that would have been that. (In fact a movie with this tunnel as its title was made about that time where the tunnel was apparently dug by shovels at a uniform depth of 30 feet below sea level. Fantasy, not science fiction.) But when the idea occurred it was then the 'sixties and readers, if not writers, were more sophisticated. All of the problem had to be looked at, not just the physical aspect. So the tunnel could be built—but *why* should it be built. Well, you know (grasping feebly at mental straws) like it's a fast way to go, no storms, save money . . . These arguments rattled away to nothing. There is no cheaper form of transport per unit mile than the bulk cargo ship. If people won't go by train from Los Angeles to New York why should they wish to cross the Atlantic in a manner other than by air? And what do you mean save money? If you did build this tunnel today you couldn't amortise the thing in under 10,000 years—if ever. Look at the fate of the Chunnel, less than one three-hundredth as long. No, it can't be done.

Not *today*. Not our today. That is the operative word in all the previous arguments against this tunnel. There must be a world in which it would be advantageous to build the thing. At this moment the plot becomes a parallel-world one, and all sorts of interesting vistas open up. There would have to be a world government, or a government so large that for all apparent purposes it could be rich enough and strong enough to do whatever it wanted. And it would have to be the same government at both ends of the tunnel. The choice—obviously—is limited to one of two. Either an American world or a British one. With a 200-year history America has not been around long enough so that history can be rearranged to make her top dog. Which leaves Britain. 1066 and all that, surely enough time to cook the historical books to put her in charge.

As this thought crossed my mind it latched firmly on to another one I had been entertaining for years. The great differences between the Spanish and the British as empire builders. I am *not* going to defend the British Raj, but I would like to point out some basic differences. Religion firstly. While the dog-collared minions of the C. of E. marched hand-in-hand with the red-coated legionaries they did not have the tremendous power for evil that was exercised by the Spanish priests and monks. Yes, suttee was banned and missions opened, and the lesser religions looked down upon as being lesser. But that was all. Throughout the pink areas of the map a thousand different religions worshipped on, and as long as they didn't cook, kill or eat people in the name of the local gods they were pretty much left alone. Not so with the Spanish Catholics. Other religions were pagan and they were taken apart. Since religion and culture were inextricably mixed with the Aztecs, Mayas and others, their societies were taken apart as well. Their histories were wiped out, their records destroyed, their places of worship defaced, their priests killed, and on and on. A very nasty job of work and a very complete one.([2]) Today Mexico, Central and South America are mongrel Spanish cultures altered only in minor cultural ways by their pre-Columbian heritage.

What would they have been like if the British, not the Spaniards, had reached them first? Would they have been more like India with a British veneer upon a native culture? The thought is an interesting one that fitted perfectly with

([2]) The valley of Toluca in Mexico was a most sacred one. There was a temple for every day of the year. The Catholics tore down 364 of them and used the stone to build churches on the site. The 365th was so big they covered it with dirt to make a hill and built a church on the summit.

the proposed British-dominated North America still in the empire. Why not South America as well? But how could this have been brought about?

The answer is in the name. Pre-Columbian. Keep Columbus away in order to give Cabot a chance. Better keep the Portuguese away as well, they were too good navigators. Where they led others would follow. The easiest way to polish them off as political entities was to slide back to a time when they didn't exist. 1492 is the operative year. This was when *los reyes Catolicos* whipped the Moors and drove them out of the Iberian peninsula, going on to unite the other Iberian states except Portugal, under the banners of Castile and Aragon, a union that would eventually form modern Spain. But this was really too late. The Moorish cause was well down the drain by 1492 and the end was pretty certain. The thing to do was to defeat the Catholic states just as they were beginning to emerge, so they could go back and brood blackly in their mountain retreats while the Moors continued to trot about on the plains below.

A happy dig through the always reliable eleventh *Encyclopedia Britannica* (no edition since this one is worth its weight in paper towels) produced the answer. The Battle of Navas de Tolosa in 1212. If the Spanish states had lost this one they could have been pushed back. And the various caliphates were still pretty much in alliance at that time.

Now the idea of the transatlantic tunnel became exciting— and possible. With the English explorers opening up all of South, Central and North America, as well as India and all the rest, the power of the empire would have been incredible. The African colonies of the other European colonists could be picked off one by one if needs be. If the European countries united early enough they might have stopped the growing British strength, but in my book they never got around to it. Divide and rule is the name of the game, so the European states still exist and monarchy is the rule, with all the royal families united —as they once were—and the power of Britain behind each one if needs be.

In the light of all this strength the American Revolution was doomed before it began, with George Washington killed as a traitor. This instantly produced the hero of the book, George's descendant who wants to clear his ancestor's name. As the game is played out more and more pieces click into place. Until, finally, the big question must be faced. Why on earth *should* they build the tunnel?

A boondoggle of course. Postulate a stagnant world with ample raw materials and great production capability—but without expanding markets. With unemployment on the rise and dole ever on the increase as well, why not find some major project that the government could back, that would make jobs and vitalise industry and get the economy plunging ahead again? Wars do this, but I am very much against war, and a lot of steel and concrete sunk on the ocean bottom is just as vanished as if it had been blown up.

Around this idea other ideas grew. This parallel world, today, would be very much like a Victorian society with certain material changes. This would have to be, in some ways, a Victorian novel. But I could not write one of these straight so it would have to be a parody or at least a humorous novel. But would it be funny in the parallel world? No! It would have to be a book written in *that* world for readers in that world. They would take it straight but readers in our world would be able to laugh at the differences. Big jokes and small became possible; the little humble Washington house beside the burned remains of Mount Vernon, the secondary characters like the detectives Richard Tracy and, a minor RBI executive, J. E. Hoover. The outline was there—but could it be fleshed out?

Unlike the producers of the movie with the similar title, I could not tunnel under the ocean until I knew what the bottom was like. The Scripps Institute of Oceanography had many thick German tomes that told me far more about the Atlantic than I cared to know. And how did one build deep water tunnels? HMSO had a three-volume report on a world-tunnelling convention with all the details I needed.

All of this was done—part-time of course!—over a five-year period. When the parts had been assembled I saw that a book could indeed be written, so contracts were signed and *A Transatlantic Tunnel, Hurrah!* was the final result. Since, early on, I had decided it would be a light book, I did not dare even touch on the real condition of the Victorian working class, child prostitution and all the various ills of society at that period. I had to ignore them. So, true to the nature of the book but not true to my own beliefs, it did turn into a Tory's vision of glory for which I do apologise to my socialist friends.

The parallel-world theme is a rich vein that has been scarcely dug into. All things are possible. In the guise of entertainment, which SF must always be primarily, many moral, physical, social, philosophical—the list is endless—problems and questions can be examined if not solved. I can only urge writers to consider the possibilities inherent in this broad theme. The readers will be satisfied I am sure because this speculative-development-thought-story is the very essence of what science fiction is all about.

6

Science Fiction and Change

ALVIN TOFFLER

ALVIN TOFFLER

Alvin Toffler is a fine and polished lecturer, with a view of the world which he believes (and I agree) it is urgently necessary to propagate. This is the view that he first outlined in his extra-ordinarily successful and influential book, *Future Shock*. It is not surprising that he does not write a complete new lecture every time (maybe ten times a week) he meets a new audience. The message does not alter radically according to its listeners.

On the other hand, he is not cynical about his audience, either. The listeners at the ICA were given ample value for money. For copyright reasons, we cannot reproduce Mr Toffler's lecture. (He made it clear that we would not be able to do this, before he accepted the engagement.) Most of his hour was devoted to the themes the general reader can find outlined in *Future Shock* and *The Eco-Spasm Report*. However, in the last few minutes he turned his attention directly to science fiction, and in that brief space of time he gave the best and most economical account of the social function of science fiction that I have ever heard. This section of his talk is reproduced below.

Incidentally, I had assumed that Mr Toffler must have been trained as a sociologist. I was delighted to learn from him that he majored in English at his university. This surely is an emblem of hope for all graduates in English (myself included) who have miserably supposed their profession in life, at best, would necessarily be to train a later generation of students to major in English, who in turn would train . . . and so on, *ad infinitum*. (And, the cynic might say, it is one in the eye for sociology.)

Despite the undoubted fact that we can trace its origins back to earlier centuries, science fiction is basically a product of the industrial revolution. This outstanding fact helps us to understand its history, its future, and the crisis in which it finds itself.

The industrial revolution provided technology, which became a major obsession of science fiction. The industrial revolution (and the Enlightenment that was so closely associated with it) provided the rationalism and optimism that for a long time powered science fiction. More important, the industrial revolution began to accelerate social and technological change to the point at which it became culturally and psychologically noticeable. Significant changes became evident within the life-span of a single individual. Thus, the future grew noticeably different from the present. And it is this divergence upon which all science fiction ultimately is based.

Today we are living through the general crisis of industrial society, the crack-up of the world produced by the industrial revolution. This creates a general crisis, as well, in all the forms we use to express our understanding of reality. And this, in turn, helps explain not merely the prevalence of identity crisis in individuals, but also the identity crisis in science fiction: uncertainty about how it fits into the cultural scheme of things; concerns about its relationship to so-called 'mainstream' literature; concerns about its relationship to fantasy and surrealism or theatre of the absurd; concerns about how it impinges on 'futurism' or 'futurology'.

If we think of today as truly revolutionary, however, as a period that will test every human capacity, then, it seems to me, science fiction has a special rôle to play in enhancing our abilities to adapt. To begin with, it forces us to question all the assumptions of the dying industrialism: assumptions about body and mind; about society, technology, politics, beauty, communication and religion.

By challenging anthropocentricism and temporal provincialism, science fiction throws open the whole of civilization and its premises to constructive criticism. Nothing is more necessary in a revolutionary moment. By dealing with possibilities not ordinarily considered—alternative worlds, alternative visions—it widens our repertoire of possible responses to change. It helps us to see the world as a system, as a whole. It helps us to think of history in very large sweeps, rather than puny slices. It also provides us with what psychologists call 'no-trial learning', that is, it permits us, as does literature in general, to test out the consequences of certain forms of behaviour, certain actions, without actually having to take those actions and the risks they entail. In societies, moreover, that do a very poor job of thinking through the second-, third- or fourth-order consequences of technology, it helps to appraise future technologies before they arrive, rather than after the fact, when it may already be too late to cope with them. At an even deeper level, science fiction tries out new epistemologies, new notions of causality, non-linear time, language and communication, and, simply by encouraging a new time-bias (a greater future-consciousness), it leads to a kind of anticipatory adaptability by the culture.

For all these reasons, I would argue that science fiction is basically pro-human, and for that I thank *you*, the writers of science fiction, for your contributions to me personally, to my rapidly transforming world, and to the future. Please don't desert tomorrow.

7

Inner Time

ALAN GARNER

ALAN GARNER

In the early planning of this lecture series, two of the subjects I had hoped to cover were 'Science Fiction and Time' and 'Science Fiction and Myth'. I invited Brian Aldiss and Samuel Delany, respectively, to speak on these subjects, and they agreed. However, circumstances changed. Brian Aldiss was desperately overworked and decided part of his trouble had been accepting too many engagements which took him away from writing his books—deserting the centre for the periphery as it were; Samuel Delany was offered a teaching post at the University of Buffalo and couldn't get away.

Then I had a moment of genius. I mentally compressed the two topics into one, and I invited Alan Garner to speak.

Alan Garner is thought of as primarily a writer of fantasies for children. It was my belief, first that his books were so strong and subtle, that it was mere foolishness to categorise him as 'a children's writer' as if by so doing we could remove him from serious consideration, just as a 'writer'; second, that (especially in the most recent novel, *Red Shift*) the word 'fantasy' suggested something very remote from the solidity and penetration of what he was actually doing—that in some ways, he was writing science fiction.

The result was the most extraordinary lecture I have ever heard. Alan Garner is not an extrovert, not a man who takes self-revelation lightly. Before the lecture he asked to be left alone. He was white-faced and tense. Giving the lecture was obviously painful. The audience could have created a nightmare situation, given the vulnerability of the lecturer, but there was no jeering, no unnecessary shifting about. They listened intently, and were clearly moved. The question period afterwards revealed how many people in the audience felt Mr Garner's lecture to have been cathartic, to have touched on areas of scarring in themselves, and allowed them to look at them. As chairman I was touched almost as much by the sensitivity and kindness of the audience as by the lecture itself.

The lecture was not what I expected. Who *could* have expected a statement as personal and powerful as this? Yet it is wholly in place in this book, for not only does it say some important things about myth and time, and the relation of science fiction to both; it says much about the most profound forces that move the writer—and without these forces, so seldom examined, we would have no science fiction—no fiction at all.

This essay describes a Western European's experience of a primitive catastrophic process, its cause and its resolution. What follows is, of necessity, subjective. Any value it may have lies in that subjectivity, and should be compared with other, objective accounts of the phenomenon, which are to be found in textbooks.

For our purposes, the experience began in the late autumn of 1968, when I adapted my own novel, *The Owl Service*, for television in eight half-hour episodes.

Translation of words into pictures is never easy, but the malaise that *The Owl Service* produced was completely unexpected; a combination of fear and exhaustion. The degree of exhaustion was debilitating, but the quality of it was worse. It was the sensation of walking unknowingly up an increasing gradient. However, the scripts were finished, and we started to film on location in April 1969, with a schedule of nine weeks

There are few occupations more tedious than the making of a film. Weather, money and time conspire to defeat the enterprise. A day's labour shows only some unrelated minutes of acting. There is no sense of dramatic progression, or even of emotional development. Filming *The Owl Service* should have rendered me inert. Instead, I felt pain, a threat from no direction, and a threat with no shape.

After a month I was regularly late for shooting each morning. My behaviour did not hold up the film, but it did undermine the director. Soon, after each take, I experienced nausea. Then I was actually sick. We were in Wales, and the other people were too busy to notice my immediate use of the nearest boulder whenever the director shouted, 'Cut!'

The next sensation was of paralysis, which never developed, and fury against the actors—which did. I could not, dare not, speak to them outside the formalities of rehearsal and shooting. 'They' were menacing, and at the same time witless.

Unhappily, one of the actors was an incompetent, and it is a tribute to the film crew that he lasted the course. But I was less professional. My unpunctuality, the nausea, the vomiting, the sense of threat—all these symptoms switched to one great symptom in the middle of a take that involved the actor.

A delicate climax of the story was being filmed, and the actor was genuinely not caring, genuinely fooling around, genuinely antagonising the cast, director and crew, and I genuinely went to kill him.

I remember leaning against one of my vomitoria, a stone wall, and seeing the daylight go out, except for a clear line round the actor's head. An animal roared inside and outside me, and I moved—but the sound engineer stuck his microphone boom between my legs and flicked me into a puddle. 'I know,' he said as he lifted me up, 'but wait till next week. We still need him.'

By the next week I was incapable of serving the film. Everybody was kind, but I had let them down. My token visits to the location were an embarrassment. I could do everything except work. But the film was finished on time, despite me, and we could all go home. June the twenty-first. The longest day.

Friends diagnosed my behaviour as nervous fatigue: I ought to take a holiday: I ought to pull myself together: I ought to relax: I ought to get away from it all. The advice was well meant: endless: useless. I could not get away from it all when 'it-all' was me.

After a sleep of several twi-lit days I entered a zombie stage. I could move about. Then I recovered, and went seemingly mad in less than three months.

The world crashed, but while there was enough of me left in command I got myself to a doctor and said that I probably needed psychiatric treatment. 'Thank goodness you asked of your own accord,' the doctor said.

Now I must appear to change the subject for a while, but the purpose is to clarify the subject beyond misrepresentation and misunderstanding, because what happened to me was something normal; yet it was superficially so close to the esoteric and to the occult that it could easily be misrepresented and misunderstood. And if 'normal' should be thought too imprecise a word, let me define it as 'that which is found to be common among a group or species'.

Having parked me in the comparatively safe orbit of a doctor's surgery, I should like to consider more generally the context of this essay. We are meant to be discussing 'science fiction'.

I use the phrase with reticence. 'Science fiction' has the sound of a botched-up job, but what it describes is an aspect of the most important function of literature, the one to which we turn in our greatest stress; that is, the flow of myth.

Man is an animal that tests boundaries. He is a 'mearc-stapa', 'boundary-strider', and the nature of myth is to help him to understand those boundaries, to cross them and to comprehend the new; so that whenever Man reaches out, it is myth that supports him with a truth that is constant, although names and shapes may change. From within us, from our past, we find the future answered and the boundary met. It may well be asked why we hold the key to questions we do not yet know, from what space and time the myth flows.

The biblical, the epic, the romantic, the gothic are all merestones, boundary-markers of their day and the pointers of ours. Three hundred years ago, the mystery was in the nearest wood; last century, the nearest grave; now, the nearest galaxy. But there are other directions, too.

What I want to state for the moment is my view that the phrase 'science fiction' is a shoddy neologism, not a new branch of story. Whether we call it the manifestation of the Jungian archetype, or the manifestation of certain human behavioural characteristics, I find in 'science fiction' the record of Man's boundary-treadings. And there will always be boundaries.

I am a writer of 'science fiction', and I have to mention my books because they are pertinent, but they need not delay us.

All are set in the present—and I would stress that. The first pair (*The Weirdstone of Brisingamen* and *The Moon of Gomrath*) I had written by the age of 27. I've dismissed them before now, especially *The Weirdstone of Brisingamen*, but recent events have made me withdraw some of my harshness.

If you look at the two books as 'science fiction' in the way I have defined the subject, they are a mess: but the germ of possibly my whole life is there. It took until 1975, and the performance of *Potter Thompson* (an opera conceived by me, and for which I wrote the libretto) to isolate the central question of those first 'boundary books' from the matrix of their self-indulgent texts. *Potter Thompson* will be discussed later.

A change came with the third book, *Elidor*. The fragmentary northern ballad of Childe Rowland and Burd Ellen was given its relevancy in the slums of Manchester. By 'relevancy' I mean that the myth chooses the form for its clearest expression at any given moment. In doing so, elements may be revealed and materials used that earlier versions obscured or did not need. For example, in describing working-class areas of the industrial north in the middle of the twentieth century, as I do in *Elidor*, I am writing no tract, but if my reporting is accurate it cannot be without sociological content. But it is not polemical or didactic writing, any more than the purpose of *Sir Gawain and the Green Knight* is to record the discomfort of sleeping rough in armour, in winter, in the middle of the fourteenth century.

The fourth novel, *The Owl Service*, is an expression of the myth found in the Welsh *Math ap Mathonwy*—and only incidentally concerned with the problems of first-generation educated illegitimate Welsh males. I labour the point because I am forced to accept that some readers will not differentiate between form and content. It is almost as if they are afraid to see.

The title of the fifth novel, *Red Shift*, prepares one for what is coming, and perhaps too much so. It may sound fictionally more scientific than it is. The myth is another ballad, the story of Tamlain and Burd Janet and the Queen of Elfland.

The element common to all the books is my present-day function within myth. The difference between that function and what are usually called 'retellings' is that the retellings are stuffed trophies on the wall, whereas I have to bring them back alive. It is a process not without risk.

It would be a mistake to call the activity plagiarism, or the bolstering of a weak imagination. I would go further, and say that the feeling is less that I choose a myth than that the myth chooses me; less that I write than that I am written.

It was from my inability to understand such a process that I appeared to go mad, but what I hope to convey is another definition; not insanity, but the conscious awareness of a dimension that the Pitjantjatra of Central Western Australia call '*Aljira*', the word usually translated as 'Dreamtime'. That is the boundary I tread. And I trod it all the way to the doctor's surgery.

We are fortunate in the part of the country where I live to have one of the most efficient psychotherapists practising today. His name, inevitably, must be Mr Smith.

The first meeting was the popular cartoonist's impression. I talked for more than two hours without interruption. Mr Smith then asked me one question. I answered it—and he went straight to the centre of pain and absolved me from it. It was a remarkable performance. We made an appointment for the following week.

Euphoria lasted, and I attended with another heap of self-revelation to wallow in. But Mr Smith would not let me start. This time I had to listen to him. And he put back (and tightened) every clamp he had removed, except the injurious one that had brought me to him. Then he dismissed me in a neutral voice which, in my confused state, sounded heartless. As soon as I was outside the building I vomited.

The next, and last, visit was a perfunctory chat, less than half an hour. He was monitoring. Then we shook hands, and I thanked him and said good-bye. 'I never say good-bye,' said Mr Smith.

So far, we have, at the very least, an impressive medical performance. I was 35 years old, and had been carrying a bomb in me for nearly 20 years, and the filming of *The Owl Service* had ignited the fuse. Mr Smith had isolated it, and dealt with it, in less than four hours of clinical time. It was a performance impressive in execution, but not unknown to orthodox science. Yet even here there are oddities.

One is that I started to lose my hold on the world during the making of the film of my own book. Writing the original book, which was four years' conscious work, had not affected me.

Another oddity is that Mr Smith, dealing with an unknown

patient who was irrational and disturbed, asked only one question the first time we met.

Mr Smith's question has implications for us all, even the most sophisticated, but especially for any artist. The question was simple, but its implications are so great that I have had to make this two-fold approach, at the risk of over-statement, in order to link the personal to the universal relevancy.

Mr Smith had asked: 'Was *The Owl Service* book written in the past tense and the third person, or in the present and the first?'

It had been written in the past tense and the third person. Although there was a lot of dialogue, it was all observed, 'he said' and 'she said', safely at a distance.

The crucial point is that an author's characters are all, to some degree, autobiographical: and the time of a film or a play is Now—dangerous as it ever was. It is here. The distance has gone.

Textbooks have a name for the disturbance, but it is a term that has been abused by popularisation and by misapplication at the hands of tendentious factions with whom I am anxious not to be associated, so that I must restore to the term its original definition before I can use it.

The word is 'engram'. An engram is, in neuro-physiology, the term for a hypothetical change in the protoplasm of the neural tissue, which is thought by some to account for the phenomenon of memory. It is a memory-trace, a permanent impression made by a stimulus or experience.

Music and smell are frequent activators of an engram. We reconstitute whole events from a line of Mozart or the scent of a flower. Psychiatry takes the matter further.

The human brain is exposed to influence from conception to death. Every event is recorded and is available to us directly—or indirectly through dreams, hypnosis or drugs. The difference between the direct and the indirect access to our files is that we usually have to surrender control of ourselves if we use the indirect methods.

Most pleasant or unhurtful experiences are put straight into their files, engrams labelled. It is the unpleasant experience that makes the threatening engram.

Here is a typical pattern for engram attack.

Something happens to us. We are hurt. We don't like being hurt. 'It' hurts. The event takes place in outer time, which is four-dimensional, and we, the organism, must continue. So, like an oyster, we enclose the pain, but, unlike the oyster, we produce no pearl. We enclose the pain by 'being sensible', 'putting it behind us', 'setting it down to experience', 'forgetting all about it'. Whatever euphemism we choose, the process is the same. We wrap the engram round with emotional energy. But the engram lives on, because the engram is a creature of inner time, and inner time is one-dimensional—or infinite. The view from outer time is unclear. All events seem to be simultaneously present: only our immediate needs give an apparent perspective. We can check the validity of this argument by calling to mind any two intensely-remembered experiences. They will be emotionally contemporaneous, even though we know that the calendar separates them by years. Similarly it is possible to reverse the calendar by comparing emotions that are not of equal strength.

An analogy may help. When we look at a starry sky, we see a group of configurations that seem to be equidistant from us and existing now. That is an 'apparent perspective'. We are looking at a complexity of times past—a sky of 'it-was', all at different epochs, distances and intensities. Inner time creates similar illusions.

The next step is a big one. Just as we are physically the result of our genetic inheritance, there are psychiatrists who see in the engram a genetic ability to transmit itself. You may say (and I *do*) that engram disorder is explicable within the subjective inner time of the individual's existence, and that that is marvel enough.

The severity of a given engram attack is related to the co-existence in inner time with all associated engrams, and their combined force threatens us. For example, we have all seen a cat that has been squashed on the road. We have seen many such cats. Now, let us suppose that on one particular day we have three equally new and equally distressing experiences—but that one of them is associated with the squashing of a cat on the road. That event will hurt us more than the other two, because it will draw on the hurt of all the cats that are being held at bay in inner time. To continue the previous analogy, the cats are a constellation of pain.

Psychiatrists who would take the matter further and say that we inherit genetically and engrammatically, hold that we have built into us the experiences of our parents from their conception to our own, and that our parents have inherited likewise from our grandparents.

It is obvious that, within a few generations of compounded inner times, the number of engrams available will approach infinity, and whether we call the result 'inherited inner time', the 'collective unconscious' or 'patterns of general human behaviour', the day-to-day result is the same. My own experience of consciously dealing with a destructive engram situation leaves me with an acceptance of the engram as a phenomenon, and of its ability to activate all its harmonics in the apparent simultaneity of inner time. But, attractive as the theory is, I have no evidence for the potential memory of what Grand-dad said in 1894.

My experience does show, however, that a writer of fiction, willy-nilly, plants encapsulated engrams in his characters, and that disorientation leading towards madness can be induced when the engram is made present simultaneously in inner and outer time.

When I assaulted the actor during the filming of *The Owl Service* it was because I could not reconcile him and me on a Welsh mountain in 1969 with the memory-trace of me somewhere else in 1950. The inner-time co-ordinates were identical, but they had been externalised to a here-and-now of waking nightmare. Inner-time rules of simultaneity and one-dimensionalism had been projected on to a four-dimensional space-time. Which was absurd. Or I was.

Mr Smith's skill lay in helping me (without drugs, hypnosis or even leading questions) to see the simplicity of the trap—that the printed word is safe where the spoken word is not. My all-but insanity was the spontaneous and ungoverned invasion of the outside world by inner time. Mr Smith showed me how to restore myself to my co-ordinates, to release the energy that had been locked round the engram for nearly 20 years, and, above all, not to be afraid of the process. That is important, because whatever words we use to describe the process, I am left with myself as someone whose function is to walk in *Aljira*, to be a vehicle of myth, to go voluntarily (and now knowingly) to inner time, and to come back increased instead of diminished, with more energy than less. And it is astonishing what can happen when our energies are not bound up defensively against an engram attack.

Before we move on, Mr Smith should be demystified. His talent is directness allied to an acute and compassionate mind. His treatment is painful because we make truth painful, and truth is the only way to discharge an engram. The method is simple. Mr Smith gets his patients to tell the pain, to tell the truth. It is often an anecdote from childhood or adolescence. He makes the patient speak always in the present tense. Not, 'I was standing in the garden', but, 'I am standing in the garden'. When the story is finished, he asks to be told the story again and again, always in the present tense, until either there is nothing left to say, or something new takes place, a deeper engram. It is like lancing a boil, or a series of boils; because the obvious engram may not be the causal engram but the final, cumulative and thereby injurious one. We may think that it is the tenth squashed cat that is hurting us, but it is more likely to be something connected with the first.

And here I must insert a warning. The simplicity of the present tense is a delusion. It is Mr Smith's skill that makes it appear simple. I am able to face fear in his presence and to take emotional risks with myself only because I know that he is medically qualified to step in with a sharp word or a sharp syringe if we meet demons. No one should be seduced into foolhardy experiments by any superficial lure in the experiences I relate.

So far, I have spoken of the engram phenomenon only as a symptom that interferes with the health of an individual. But the positive side is equally available, though we tend not to draw on it. Primitive peoples do; and 'primitive' is not the same as 'unsophisticated'.

Inner time may not exist, as such. It may be a confusion on my part from many sources, but it is an empirical truth for me, from which I am led to *believe* that Man is evolving, through that inner time as well as through others, towards awareness of a universe that is conscious rather than effete. And to be conscious is to be responsible: to be responsible is to act: to act is to move: for ever.

Up till now I have given an account of a situation that is behind me. The intervening years have been filled with activity made possible by the discharge of a crippling engram, and here are some of the results.

Immediately 'after' being treated clinically by Mr Smith, I organised the dismantling, repair and re-erection of the most important timber-framed Tudor domestic building known to have survived; had it linked to the existing medieval hall-house where I live; filmed and photographed the operation, and handled the archaeological complexities involved. (The medieval hall-hovel is on a Saxon/Iron Age/Beaker/Neolithic site.)

I wrote *Red Shift*; made a television documentary film; wrote a television play; conceived and wrote the libretti for two operas; collaborated on a picture book for children; wrote a dance drama; wrote a study of a Jungian archetype; got married again; fathered a child; am monitoring another pregnancy; am working on three stage plays and another for television; am editing a series of biographies; am collaborating on an analysis of a Middle-English poem; am preparing one of the operas for filming on television and for stereo recording on radio; am devising a new libretto; am researching six documentary films; am writing a short story; am mulling over the problems of writing original material for cassette recordings; and am gestating the next novel. I feel under-employed.

In the fourteen years of work before my collapse, I wrote four novels, and did sporadic radio and television jobs in order to eat.

Surely it cannot be a coincidence that so much should happen as soon as the energy needed to sit on an engram for nearly 20 years was made available for more constructive, outwardly-turned activities.

And, because I have long maintained that war memoirs are not as truthful as despatches from the front, I have set out to demonstrate, in the only way I know how, that there need not be anything too terrible about what still has to be called 'mental illness' by writing this essay in the twelfth week of another crisis; one caused by an engram in the opera *Potter Thompson*. The whole opera was itself a theatrical expression of engram resolution and the nature of inner time, and I am still reverberating.

It is not a sick joke, but there is a joke. For what I am, and what Mr Smith does, in other societies is seen quite differently.

To the shamans of Turukhansk I should not fulfil their recruiting standards. Potential shamans are looked for among epileptic children and the severely disturbed, including those suffering from schizophrenia and other psychoses.

The chosen initiates are subjected to years of tuition in the sacred rites of the community, the mastery of all arts, the memorising of epics, the knowledge of medicine and the control of trance states. At the end of the process, the now adults (who, in our world, would be lobotomised, sedated or rejected) are the spiritual leaders of their people. Many would still be diagnosed as epileptic, severely disturbed, psychotic—but with an inexplicable difference. They manifest their symptoms under the control of their will, in the service of their community, to heal the sick and to communicate with God. There are no involuntary seizures, no social problems. The individual has a place. He is of the elect, an asset not an embarrassment.

Now I have just given a summary of the main activities that occupy me at present, and contrasted them with the aridity of what went before. You may find both states unhealthy and ludicrous. But we are individuals, and it is not in me to be equable. The choice is only of which whirlwinds to ride. Given that, I am told my work is richer now, less diffused, and that I am more tolerable domestically. The involvement of an academically-trained Western mind with a primitive catastrophic process (that is, the waking experience of *Aljira*, Dreamtime, the *Illud Tempus* of anthropology) is not always pleasant, but it is never far from what C. S. Lewis calls 'Joy', and I would have it no other way.

I may still write only another four novels in the next fourteen years. It is the interstitial energy that is revealing. I can now fill the gaps with movement, film, music, possibly even scholarship—and stay human, and become humane. Consider what energy those activities represent: turn that energy so that it implodes. There is the hell of zero.

Let me return to the opera *Potter Thompson*. I have devoted a lot of space here to engrams, but have not described the subjective experience of discharging one; the road back from zero.

As with the filming of *The Owl Service*, when *Potter Thompson* was about to go into rehearsal—that is, to get off the page and to take on flesh—I began to apply my brakes in the form of psychosomatic malaise.

My wife told me I should see Mr Smith, but I ignored the advice. After all, he was for the big stuff, not backache and migraine. And anyway, I was 'busy'. Then one night I shouted in my sleep, 'I wrote the thing! I don't have to watch it!' When I heard what had happened I scrapped the arguments for not needing help, but before I could get to Mr Smith the brakes were jammed on. Everything that had ever ached, ached. Each preparation for the journey to London produced another batch of symptoms, until I woke to find I could not get out of bed. Hysterical paralysis had taken all the pains away. That made me angry, angry enough to load myself into a car to keep my appointment with Mr Smith. But the session started with me in ridiculous contortion on the floor because of muscular spasm, and barely able to speak.

Here is how it went. The dialogue is bizarre, especially out of context, but remember that Mr Smith and I had worked together and accepted a shorthand vocabulary between us concerned with effectiveness rather than with elegance.

'Go to the pain,' said Mr Smith. 'Go to where it hurts most, and say whatever it tells you.'

The centre of the pain was my left thigh. I zoomed in like a camera lens, crashing for the black centre, using my will as a projectile. Just before the moment of impact, the blackness switched off, and I was watching myself, six years old, at home, during the war, being sick after eating the top half of a teacake covered with blackcurrant jam—and developing the first symptoms of what was later diagnosed as spinal and cerebral meningitis.

Engram One. I told the story over and over, in the present tense, until nothing was left that was unpleasant—except the teacake.

'Go to the most painful part of that experience, and say whatever it tells you.'

Again the crash zoom lens—into the teacake. And immediately another picture, another associated memory, a deeper engram.

A peculiarity of this technique is that, instead of becoming more tedious with each repetition, the description is more vivid, visually and emotionally (and therefore more painful and diffi-cult), until there is a sudden loss of intensity, and the engram is discharged: but it is not erased.

The engram makes no distinction between an actual experi-ence (one that we could photograph and record objectively) and a dream. The more dream-engrams there are, the more painful the process and the sooner the resolution. Also, the engram prefers the emotional truth to the historical truth, so that it does not matter if one is 'lying' in the sense of untruthful evidence before a court of law, since we are dealing with the subjective truth of the pain in order to free it here-and-now: we are not conducting an experiment to test the accuracy of human memory and its retention. But the usual pattern is to move from historical event to historical event, sometimes taking shortcuts through truth and remembered dream. Puns are common, too.

After two hours of the first session I walked out with a sore leg.

We chased engrams all that week, until I crash zoomed into the last of the series, and found myself screaming, aged three, being carried by an usherette from my first visit to a cinema. Nobody had explained what a film was, let alone an animated cartoon, and I had sat in the largest enclosed space of my life, in the dark, and watched something fifteen feet high, moving and coloured. It was the film of *Snow White*. I broke at the metamorphosis of the queen to the witch. My mother stayed behind to watch the rest of the film.

I was thrashed when we got home, for making my mother 'look a fool in public'.

'Go to the most painful part of the experience.'

'Waiting with Mummy after the film, before we get home.'

'Where are you waiting?' said Mr Smith.

'At a bus-stop.'

'Isn't it a funny old world?' said Mr Smith. 'What do you feel now?'

'I want to be in London, so they don't foul up the opera.'

'You'll still have a pain in your leg,' said Mr Smith. 'It's sciatica.'

And it is sciatica. But if I swear at it, it goes. I can will it away. In another century, I should have been casting out a devil.

Whatever terminology we use, it is a fact that from my hysterical paralysis and fear of watching *Potter Thompson*, to wanting to be rid of a psychotherapist because he was delaying my arrival at rehearsal, and all in five days, was an achievement.

It should also be noticed that Mr Smith called a temporary halt and sent me to experience *Potter Thompson* as soon as I mentioned that the most distressing aspect of the *Snow White* engram was my standing at a bus-stop, afraid of what had happened, afraid of the thrashing to come, and denied my mother's affection in the present. It was a one-dimensional point of fear.

And when I first met Mr Smith, when the world was crashing, and the personal pain was greater and its social effect a near disaster, we chased an engram and discharged it: but only one. One engram for the edge of collapse, five engrams for sciatica. But there is a connection, and it is reasonable.

The Owl Service was written largely from a need to understand why, at the age of fifteen, I had, without justification or desire, verbally savaged another human being. I had done it at a bus-stop. That was the centre of pain that Mr Smith went to and from which he absolved me. 'The bus-stop' was the engram I had not been able to recognise or discharge on a Welsh mountain.

When I was seventeen, the tables were turned on me by someone else in a similar way, and out of that bewilderment came the need to write *Elidor*. It happened, of course, at a bus-stop.

Even the first books, *The Weirdstone of Brisingamen* and *The Moon of Gomrath*, have bus-stops within them—and they are based on the myth that is expressed through *Potter Thompson*.

Let us be clear, and remember the squashed cats. Three equally painful experiences happen to me on the same day, but one involves the squashing of a cat; and therefore all the squashed cats of my inner time bleed—and if the engram has a genetic ability to transmit itself, the cats of my grandsires bleed, too. I do not doubt that I behaved intolerably to many other human beings, and they to me: but I retain negatively and destructively only the bus-stop experiences, because they had the additional charge upon them of my infant terror and the withholding of parental love; which made me too cruel and then too vulnerable in my turn.

It's a funny old world only here-and-now. For inner time, what I have described is that quarrelsome word 'normality'.

It seems to me that one motivation for a writer could be the need to discharge engrams. If it were as easy as that, writers would end up as saints, but fortunately there are too many engrams and too little life—and it will do no good to look for engrams cold, because any you dig out will be bogus, and so will you. Which is why, at our first meeting, Mr Smith went only as far as the pain took me. I imagine that he could have forced me to more bus-stops, out of interest, but he is a sensitive man. He knew what those 20 years had done, and that I needed to make up lost time, and that it would be soon enough to help me further when the next stage was reached. 'I never say good-bye' was his signal to be remembered when the need came.

By implication, there is something behind the first bus-stop, but I am not ready for it yet. When I can deal with it, then it will emerge, and I shall be a little further on my journey.

The discharge of an engram through writing may be an act of exorcism, but it is not confessional writing. If it succeeds, I am not giving the reader the burden of my engram, but I am fortuitously handing on the released, and thereby refined and untainted, energy. Again, I could not do it cold, or with a social mission: I am not Galahad: but it is astonishing (and humbling) to read my mail and to have people say simply, 'Thank you': and then to realise that they have taken something beneficial from a process that has been in me since before they were born, a process that has been discharged through me, so that my bad 1949 becomes an unknown person's good 1975.

The danger of hubris is clear, but it is countered by the certain belief that if that process were abused or manipulated I should be destroyed, and by the cosmic joke of my own work. For there is not one problem sweated out clinically with Mr Smith that I have not already myself posited, examined and resolved earlier in a book.

I got to London for *Potter Thompson* through dealing with a conflict that is answered in detail by the last chapter of *The Owl Service*, which was written nine years earlier. However long a book may occupy, living the truth of it takes longer.

The present exercise with Mr Smith is all laid out in *Potter Thompson*. I can even see where I am now, what must be done, and what the result will be. But I do not know yet how to do it. To reach the catharsis of my personal *Potter Thompson* I shall have to write a stage play, a libretto and a novel. And what will they uncover? And what will it take to answer?

The answer already exists in myth. If I have made the engram phenomenon seem hard, it is because evolution is hard, and we must evolve. I believe that we are evolving towards a hyper-consciousness of the individual, and that one of the evolutionary processes is concerned with inner time, a potential we are made aware of by the action of myth. At certain times in life, especially in adolescence, the potential universe is open to our comprehension, and it is not the engram's fault if we decide to be blind to the light and call on darkness.

The engram is not harmful, unless we ignore it. I have described no mystery that is not of our own making, no fear that is outside us. In other cultures there would be no need for explanation. But we are not other cultures, and I have no wish to enter *Aljira* as a Pitjantjatra, but as a twentieth-century Western European, with all my cultural skills intact.

The analogy of a starry sky may help us finally to understand what I mean.

The Pitjantjatra live in Australia, now: but technologically they are 20,000 years in our past. Their ingenuity of survival in a desert where we should not last a day is a product of the application of *Aljira, Illud Tempus*, inner time, myth, to their environment. The numinous quality of Man is dominant in them.

But take a tribal Pitjantjatra and expose him to our technology, and he dies. He is no longer tribal, he has no co-ordinates. An individual who can cross the Dead Centre of Australia naked, cannot cross Sydney alone. He hits skid row instead.

The simultaneity of the Pitjantjatra and ourselves is another 'apparent perspective', like the sky, and is what makes geno-cides of missionaries.

Somewhere in those 20,000 years we sacrificed the numinous for our other greatness—the intellect. The mistake has been to atrophy our dreams.

My intellect entered inner time as unprepared as a Pitjant-jatra entering Sydney. But I survived, and have returned the better equipped to work. For now I know that whatever that work is, comes through me, not from me, and brings with it a proper pride, a pride in craft, not the hubristic pride of creation.

And I have no choice but to serve that work—not only with the numinous aspect of Man, for which I make this plea, but with the intellectual and analytical force that is our history, and by which we move thought through outer space and outer time to other minds.

The boundaries are endless. But we each have our function. Perhaps the artist's job is to act as cartographer for all navi-gators, and I simply plot the maps of inner stars.

8

The Embarrassments of Science Fiction

THOMAS M. DISCH

THOMAS M. DISCH

Tom Disch is one of the finest, most subtle and probably most generally undervalued writers of science fiction today. Three of his strongest books—for the benefit of any reader who is not familiar with Disch's work—are the early *The Genocides* and the recent *334*, and the short story collection *Getting Into Death*. He is that unusual thing in science fiction, an ironist, whose writing voice blends something of the dry wit of a New Yorker (which he is) and the experienced, unsurprised eye of the European. (He has lived for long periods in England and Italy.)

He read his lecture, with an apology, from a prepared text, which appears below without a word changed. It was a refreshing if alarming experience to hear him lay into so many of the sacred cows of science fiction, hardly pausing to wipe the blood from his blade before turning to the next victim. The operation had no air of guilt about it, no artificial working up into a frenzy by donning his bear-skin and biting the rim of his shield. He is a tall, solidly built man with a cheery manner, and he did his job much as a worker in the Chicago Meat Yards might, with jovial pride in a job well done, except that he chose the rapier rather than the electric stun-gun.

By one of those coincidences which I find a cheerful, if misleading, token of some great universal pattern, Tom Disch chose to make a number of points which related closely to those I knew I would be making myself in the following lecture. We had never previously met, so there was no collusion. Fortunately, it seemed to me, I would not be so much repeating Disch's points as complementing them, homing in on some of the same areas in a different context and with a different tone. None the less, I certainly found myself appearing to echo some of his judgements. I hope that readers accept this as a sign that the judgements are valid, rather than an emblem of editorial incapacity or, worse, plagiarism.

Embarrassment is in itself an embarrassing subject. Like beauty, it is all too apt to have its source in the sensibility of the beholder. Why should I be made uneasy by someone else's faults unless I fear to see my own mirrored in them. A capacity for embarrassment implies, at the very least, a lack of that loftiness and high cool that we all try to pretend is natural to us. No one, for instance, blushes at the blunders in a school play, for it is easy to see children, even one's own, in their eternal aspect. The point of having them on stage is for the charm of their inevitable failure in filling out their grown-up rôles. If it were, instead, one's husband or wife who were so publicly failing, embarrassment would be hard to avoid—though there might still be charm for others in the audience.

Sophistication requires one to have no friends, or only those who can be counted on either never to fail or never to venture forth. In the quintessentially sophisticated world of Proust's novels there are no moments of embarrassment: his artists are first-rate, his aristocrats know better than to *do* anything, and everyone else is a provincial. A provincial is any person who *would* be embarrassing if he were a friend or a member of the same club.

Science fiction writers are provincials of literature. We have always been able to embarrass each other, but to the world at large our gaucheries are generally accounted a major (if not the entire) part of our charm. The critic Leslie Fiedler could end a speech in praise of science fiction with the sincere hope that SF should not lose 'its slapdash quality, its sloppiness, or its vulgarity'. So might a countess lavish praise on the ruddy health and unaffected manners of milkmaids. Samuel Delany wrote a long and satisfying essay taking Fiedler to task for his condescensions and pointing out that milkmaids acquire their complexions and their fetching rags as a consequence largely of the conditions they must work in and the pay they receive. I can't do better, by way of moving on, than to quote Delany: 'Slapdash writing, sloppiness, and vulgarity are, no matter how you catch them, fat, diseased lice.'

So much for our relations with the mainstream. While we remain provincials, it will not be possible to command any other kind of attention from the capitals of art. It is for us to take ourselves seriously and to consider the uncomfortable question of whether we ought to be permitted out into company. Many of the failings of provincials—their clothes, their manners, their accents—are easily correctable or else forgiveable, but others, such as ignorance and complacency, are rooted in the provincial condition. My purpose in this essay is to consider the degree to which science fiction has its source in its own most flagrant faults.

Late in 1970 I made a suggestion, in the bulletin of the Science Fiction Writers of America, that I thought satisfactorily accounted for most of what was radically wrong with SF, as well as a good part of what was right. I suggested that science fiction is a branch of children's literature.

Let me count the ways.

In my own case, and in that of almost all my contemporaries who admit to a taste for it, that taste was acquired at around age thirteen. Often earlier; seldom much later than fifteen (though I have met a woman of mature years who became an avid reader of SF at age 40, during a long period of hospitalisation). The taste may persist throughout life, but it seldom again exercises the addictive force it possesses in early adolescence, except among science fiction fans (concerning whom I shall have more to say by and by).

Consider, too, how many classic novels and stories in the genre are about children of exceptional wisdom and power. There was an early anthology, *Children Of Wonder*, which I doted on, devoted to this sole theme. There are, as well, Van Vogt's *Slan*, Sturgeon's *More Than Human*, Wyndham's *The Chrysalids* (*Re-Birth* in America), Pangborn's *A Mirror For Observers*, and major novels by Clement, Clarke, Asimov, and Blish—in all of which the protagonists are children. May it not be safely assumed that one reason for this is that such books were written *for* children?

To say that a book is written for children is not a condemnation, of course, but it is a limitation. It is limiting intellectually, emotionally, and morally. To consider those limitations in that order:

The intellectual limitations of SF are the more remarkable by virtue of the degree to which many of its readers and writers seem to regard their involvement with the genre as a badge of intellectual distinction, like a membership in Mensa. This sorts oddly with an engrained anti-intellectualism and repeated demands that SF should stick to its last and provide only escapist entertainment—and yet many of the elder statesmen of the field are capable of such seeming self-contradictions. In fact, if they could but state it, their position is demonstrably consistent, and in fact, like all our opinions, is essentially a rationalisation of their practice. Briefly, they would allow writers to deal speculatively with whatever materials might be introduced into a beginning course in the physical sciences, while disbarring irony, aesthetic novelty, any assumption that the reader shares in, or knows about, the civilisation he is riding along in, or even a tone of voice suggesting mature thoughtfulness. SF obeying these rules is called hard-core SF, and some purists would have it that it is the only kind that matters. A classic hard-core story, many times reprinted, Tom Godwin's "The Cold Equations" concerns an eighteen-year-old girl stowaway on a space ship, who must be jettisoned because in calculating the fuel needed for landing no allowance has been made for her additional mass. Much is made of the fact that at an acceleration of five gravities the girl's one-gravity weight of 110 pounds will increase to an effective 550 pounds. As a specimen of English prose, of character portrayal, of sociological imagination, the story can only be judged as puerile; yet within its own terms, as a fable designed to convey to very young people that science is not a respecter of persons, it is modestly successful.

The emotional limitations of children's literature are even more restrictive. There are, here and there, children bright enough to cope with the *Scientific American* or even the *Times Literary Supplement*, but crucial aspects of adult experience remain boring even to these prodigies. At the cinema children fail to see the necessity for love scenes, and if a whole movie were to prove to be about nothing else, then they would just as soon not sit through it. No less an authority than Kingsley Amis has pronounced sex and love as being outside the sphere of interest proper to science fiction. Other subjects commonly dealt with by mainstream writers are also presumed not to be of interest to SF readers, such as the nature of the class system and the real exercise of power within that system. Although there is no intrinsic reason (except difficulty) that SF should not venture into such areas, SF writers have characteristically preferred imaginary worlds in which, to quote Sprague de Camp, 'all men are mighty, all women beautiful, all problems simple, and all life adventuresome'.

The moral limitations of a literature built on such premises should be immediately apparent. Evil is seen as intrinsically external, a blackness ranged against the unvaried whites of heroism. Unhappy endings are the outcome of occasional cold equations, not of flawed human nature. There can be no tragic dimension of experience. Even a tentative expression of pessimism is regarded as grounds for dismissing a work out of hand. Compare SF to mysteries in this respect. Every mystery, however misbegotten, assumes that men are all capable of any degree of evil. That is, all characters are suspects. Such an assumption is essentially foreign to the experience of children. This is not to say that children are innocent, but only that they suppose they are.

Having put forward these reasons for considering SF to be a branch of children's literature, I must confess that something essential remains lacking—chiefly, an explanation of why it is read by so many adults. Further, science fiction has other failings and limitations that this theory fails to account for. I am left with an interesting and only partially valid observation, whose chief merit is that it has been a small annoyance to various people I don't like.

Let me approach the problem from a different direction—the problem, that is, of who reads SF and why. And let me explain, as a kind of belated preface, why the nature of science fiction's readership is so crucial a consideration.

Genre fiction may be distinguished from other kinds of

writing in being shaped by the (presumed) demands of its audience rather than by the creative will of its writers. The writers accommodate their talents to the genre's established formulae. These formulae exist in order to guarantee readers the repetition of pleasures fondly remembered. It is no more reprehensible for a writer to seek to gratify such expectations than for a restaurant to do so; and it may be done, in one case as in the other, with more or less skill. This emphasis on replication rather than creation does explain why cookery—and hack writing—finally must be considered as crafts rather than as arts. Indeed, the very mention of 'art' is apt to bring a manly sneer to the lips of the hack writer, who prides himself on his craftsmanship, his competence as an entertainer meeting the demands of an audience. It follows that we may learn more about any genre by examining its readership than by studying its writers.

As an example of such an approach, let me quote an article in which I sought to account for the conventions of the gothic romance.

Gothics [I wrote] are mostly read by housewives or those who see a life of housewifery looming ahead. In gothics the heroine is mysteriously threatened and wonders whether it was her husband/fiancé who tried to drop the chandelier on her . . . Few of the ladies who devour gothics are in serious danger of being pushed off a cliff in Cornwall for the sake of their legacies, yet the analogue of the brand of fiction they buy to their real predicament is close. Every gothic reader must ask herself whether her marriage is worth the grief, the ritual insincerity, the buried rancour, and the sacrifice of other possibilities that every marriage entails. To which the gothic writer replies with a resounding Yes! It *is* worth all that because down deep he really does love you. Yet to the degree that this answer rings hollow the experience must be renewed. Poor Eleanor must return to the dark castle of her doubts, and the doubts must be denied. And then again.

Is there an analogous model of the representative reader for the much broader and more complex genre of science fiction?

I believe there are probably several. One such might be a precocious fourteen year old, impatient with his education, anxious for economic independence, with a highly-developed faculty for day-dreaming and little emotional or moral sophistication concerning the content of his daydreams. That is a fairly accurate portrait of myself at age fourteen, when my passion for SF had reached its height. Now, not just any day-dream will serve for such a reader. It must be one to suit his circumstances. Try this, for instance. I quote from the back cover of a paperback:

> Somewhere in this world there are six people who—together —can do anything. Some day, perhaps tomorrow, they will put their power to work and the world will be transformed. In the meantime they are waiting quietly. They look—and often behave—like people you know. But with a difference: they think of themselves as 'I'—not 'we'—because in a curious way they are One.

Add to this that the central figure of the book is a schoolboy of prodigious intellectual gifts desperately trying to pass himself off on the world as the boy next door. This book, as every SF reader will recognise, is Theodore Sturgeon's *More Than Human*. It is a book that even today I cannot praise highly enough. Among its many excellences is the fact that it uses its considerable power *as a daydream* to inculcate ethical values and spiritual insights usually entirely absent from genre writing. For instance, the book's insistence on mutual inter-dependency (and, by implication, on psychic integration) is in sharp contrast to the legion of stories in which the hero discovers the fate of the world to rest in his sole power. Another theme of the book—the need to bide one's time—is of obvious utility to any fourteen year old. But the largest subliminal lesson is latent in the fantasy of possessing secret mental powers. What this represents, I believe, is an assurance that there *is* a world of thought and inner experience of immense importance and within everybody's grasp. But it is only there for those who cultivate it.

So long as one stands in need of such assurances and exhorta-tions, so long will SF remain a source of solace and of strength.

That is why SF is *par excellence* the literature of students, and why, usually, once you've got your degree and begun to lead a livelier life in the wider world, your need for the intellectual cheerleaders of SF slackens. However, if for any reason you don't get the degree, or if the degree doesn't get you what you thought it would, then you may be doomed to spin the wheel of this one fantasy forever. These, the second especially, are large qualifications. Few expectations worth the having are likely to be entirely fulfilled, and so there remains in every foolish heart appetites that only fantasy can assuage.

That is one model of the science fiction reader, and essentially it is an elaboration of my first theory—that SF is written for children. There is, however, another kind of science fiction reader, more typical formerly than now, who is drawn to the genre by distinctly different needs. His preference is for a different sort of SF than that I've been considering till now. He regards the Golden Age of SF as the 'thirties and 'forties. He is an admirer of E. E. Smith, of Edgar Rice Burroughs, of A. E. van Vogt, and, at the farthest stretch of his imagination, of Robert Heinlein This is the science fiction 'fan', and he exercises, by the preponderant and inarguable weight of his purchases, a major influence on the genre.

Since I cannot frame a description of this reader in terms that do not betray my bias against him, I should like to defer to John W. Campbell, Jr., who in 1952 wrote this description of his conception of the average reader of his magazine, *Astounding*:

> Reader surveys show the following general data: that the readers are largely young men between 20 and 35, with a scattering of younger college students, and older professional technical men; and that nearly all the readers are technically trained and employed.
>
> The nature of the interest in the stories is not economic, not love, but technical-philosophical.

Now, as an example of what Campbell's technically-trained élite was enjoying in those days in the pages of *Astounding*, I'd like to quote a brief passage from A. E. van Vogt's *The World Of Null-A*, which Campbell has called 'One of those once-in-a-decade classics'. In this passage the hero and his girlfriend

have gone to a giant computer to be tested in their understanding of the principles of a new all-purpose science called
General Semantics.

> 'Now that I'm here,' said Teresa Clark, 'I'm no longer so
> sure of myself. Those people look darned intelligent.'
>
> Gosseyn laughed at the expression on her face, but he
> said nothing. He felt supremely positive that he could
> compete right through to the thirtieth day. His problem
> was not would he win, but would he be allowed to try.

The story proves his doubts to be justified, for he is beset
on all sides by mysterious and implacable enemies. Thanks,
however, to his grasp of non-Aristotelian logic he does win
through. Concerning the virtues of this new philosophy, van
Vogt had this to say in his introduction:

> Every individual scientist is limited in his ability to abstract
> data from Nature by the brainwashing he has received from
> his parents and in school. As the General Semanticist would
> say, each scientific researcher 'trails his history' into every
> research project. Thus, a physicist with less educational or
> personal rigidity can solve a problem that was beyond the
> ability (to abstract) of another physicist.

What can be inferred of a reader for whom van Vogt's
sentiments and the situations of his fiction are persuasive?
First, I think, that education is a subject of profound ambiva-
lence. On the one hand success is equated with passing a test
administered by a computer that shares the author's reverence
for non-Aristotelian logic. There is some apprehension as to
one's competitors, for they look 'darned intelligent'. On the
other hand, we (of the real world) are apparently 'brainwashed'
in school, and physicists with *less* education may be better
qualified to solve certain problems than their better-educated
peers. While I have my own reservations about the educational
system, there is a ring for me, through all of this, of dead-end
jobs and correspondence schools (whose come-ons regularly
grace the back covers of SF magazines). The technical training
and employment that Campbell speaks of are all too often

likely to be training in the use of the soldering iron or even the crowbar. Van Vogt and Campbell speak all too clearly the language of lower-middle-class aspiration and resentment, nor are they alone in this. By far the greater part of all pulp science fiction from the time of Wells till now was written to provide a semi-literate audience with compensatory fantasies.

This aspect of the social origins and provenance of SF, though seldom spoken of, will not come as a surprise to the seasoned reader of the genre. The pulp magazines that arose at the turn of the century had, as a matter of survival, to cater to the needs of the newly literate working classes. Inevitably, it shows.

SF is rife with fantasies of powerless individuals, of ambiguous antecedents, rising to positions of commanding importance. Often they become world saviours. The appeal of such fantasies is doubtless greater to one whose prevailing sense of himself is of being undervalued and meanly employed; who believes his essential worth is hidden under the bushel of a life that somehow hasn't worked out as planned; whose most-rooted conviction is that he is capable of *more*, though as to the nature of this unrealised potential he may not be too precise.

Another prominent feature of SF that is surely related to the naïve character of its audience is its close resemblance, often bordering on identity, with myth, legend and fairy tales. Throughout the twentieth century a large part of the American urban lower classes, from which the SF audience was drawn, were recent immigrants from what is commonly called the Old Country—that is to say, from the place where folk tales were still a living tradition. Indeed, except for the stories of their religions, this was likely to have been the only literary tradition familiar to these immigrants. Thus, few of the first SF readers were more than a generation away from the oral tradition at its most traditional. Think of that sense of wonder that is the touchstone of the early pulp stories: could it not be, in essence, an analogue of the sense of wonder all country mice experience at their first view of a modern metropolis? Doubtless, the twentieth century has had some surprises even for sophisticated city mice but it is part of *their* code not to let on to this. Surely they will not erect wonder, novelty, and the massive suspension of disbelief into first principles of their aesthetics. Sophisticates require the whole complex apparatus developed by two centuries of realistic novelists in order just to begin enjoying a made-up story. But for a naïve audience, as for children, it is enough to say 'Once there was a city made all of gold', and that city rises up in all its simple splendour before their inner eye.

A less beguiling feature we may expect to find in a lower-class literature is resentment. Resentment, because it has its source in repressed anger, usually is expressed in indirect forms. Thus, the chief advantage of the ruling classes, their wealth and the power it provides, is dealt with in most science fiction by simply denying its importance. Power results from personal virtue or the magic of machines. It is rather the personal characteristics of the wealthy that become the focus of the readers' resentment—their cultivated accents, their soft hands, their preposterous or just plain incomprehensible ideas, which they refuse to discuss except by their own ornate rules in their own tiresome language. Most maddeningly, they hold the unswervable and utterly unfair conviction that because they've had the good luck to be better educated they are therefore smarter. In a world full of doltish university graduates, this assumption of superiority is in the highest degree exasperating to any moderately intelligent machinist or clerk. But what is to be done? To attempt to catch up could be the work of a lifetime, and at the end of it one has only succeeded in becoming a poor copy of what one originally despised—an effete intellectual snob.

Happily, or unhappily, there is an alternative. Deny outright the wisdom of the world and be initiated to a secret wisdom. Become a true believer—it matters not the faith, so long as it is at variance with *theirs*. All millennialist religions have their origins in this need for creating a *counter*-culture. As religion loses its unique authority, almost any bizarre set of beliefs can become the focus of a sense of Election. Whatever the belief, the rationale for it is the same: the so-called authorities are a pack of fools and frauds with minds closed to any but their own ideas. Just because they've published books doesn't mean a thing. There are other books that are in complete opposition. Beginning with such arguments, and armed with the right book, one may find one's way to almost any conclusion one might take a fancy to: hollow earths, Dean drives, the descent of mankind from interstellar visitors. For the more energetic true believer there are vaster systems of belief, such as Scientology. I select these examples from the myriad available because each historically has been a first cousin of science fiction. And for this good reason: that SF is a virtual treasury of ways of standing the conventional wisdom on its head. Only sophisticates will make a fine distinction between playing with ideas and adopting them. For a naïve reader the imaginative excitement engendered by a new notion easily crystallised into faith.

As this begins to sound like an indictment of SF and its readers, I should like to point out that these class-associated features of SF should not be considered as faults. They are essentially neutral and may be employed to good or ill effect, according to the gifts and good will of any given writer. Fantasies of power are a necessary precondition of the exercise of power—by anyone. One cannot do what one hasn't first imagined doing. The upper classes possess a great initial advantage in discovering while still young that the world is in essential agreement with *their* fantasies of power. Princes have a great resource of self-confidence in knowing that some day they'll be kings. Self-help books, from Samuel Smiles through Dale Carnegie, all agree on the crucial importance of hyping yourself into a state of self-confidence. Without that there is little chance of competing against the toffs, who got their gleaming teeth and firm handshakes, as it were, by inheritance. As a device for schooling the mind in what it feels like to be a real go-ahead winner, a few novels by Edgar Rice Burroughs could be quite as effective as an equivalent dosage of Positive Thinking. To denigrate the power fantasies of SF is very like laughing at cripples because they use crutches. A crutch that serves its purpose is to be admired.

As to the kinship between SF and fairy tales and legends, I should not think it would be necessary to make apology. What more fertile soil could any fiction sink its roots into, after all? If individual artists have not always been equal to their materials, that is their loss. It is our gain as readers that often, even so, their botched tales retain the power to astonish us. Even in a cheap frankfurter pork tastes good.

Finally as to resentment, who shall say that there are not often enough good grounds for it? Anger and defiance may be healthier, manlier modes of expression, but when the way to these is barred, we must make do somehow. "Cinderella" and "The Ugly Duckling" are fantasies inspired by resentment, and they possess an undeniable, even archetypal, power. When we are compelled to recognise that our allegiance is owing to powers, whether parents or presidents, whose character is flawed or corrupt, what shall we feel in acquiescing to those powers (as we all do, sometimes) unless resentment? The lower classes may feel their oppression more keenly because it is more immediate and pervasive, but resentment to some degree is part of the human condition.

However (and alas) this does not end the matter. Resentment may be universal, but it is also universally dangerous, for the political programme of the resentful inevitably savours of totalitarianism and a spirit of revenge. Once they attain to political power the know-nothings can have a sweet triumph over the know-it-alls by *declaring* that the earth is flat, or Einstein a heretic. The books of one's enemies can be burned or re-edited. I am by no means the first to observe and deplore this fact of political life, nor yet to note its bearing on a certain variety of science fiction. For a fuller consideration of the fascism lurking beneath the smooth chromium surface of a good deal of SF, I recommend Adolf Hitler's remarkable novel, *Lord Of The Swastika*, also known as *The Iron Dream* by Norman Spinrad.

This aspect of SF is only alarming to the degree that the jack-booted variety of SF writer can make good their claim to speak for the field as a whole: which today, surely, is far from being the case. However, this side of SF does remain an embarrassment so long as SF is regarded as a unitary phenomenon, an extended family whose members have a general obligation to notice each other's existence. In the larger world of mainstream literature, matters are ordered otherwise. The better sort of writers simply ignore the productions of their inferiors, even as they crowd their own off the best-seller lists. They do this in much the same way that the gentry arrange their lives so as to be able to ignore the scowling faces of the lower orders. This has its inequities, as when good writers have the misfortune to be tagged as 'popular entertainers' and fail to receive the critical attention their work merits. But it is undeniably a convenient arrangement, and for good or ill, it is happening right now to SF. It is stratifying into the same three-deck arrangement of highbrow, middle-brow, and lowbrow. A new variety of reader has sprung up beside the older fandom and the ever-replenished ranks of juvenile readers. This new readership has its own distinctive needs and preferences. Being one of the trees, my own view of the forest is not necessarily to be trusted, and so I will not try to characterise these readers, except to call them—*us*. My only reason for bringing up the matter at all is to pose the question of what *our* relation to *them* should be.

In my first notes for this speech I had a kind of half-aphorism that I haven't been able to sneak in anywhere along the way. It was this: SF bears the same relation to fiction that Scientology bears to science. It works for some, but it won't bear looking at. Essentially the question that remains to be asked is whether such a statement—that it won't bear looking at—is justifiable or wise. When it is said that the poor shall always be with us, too often the implication is that one may therefore ignore the poor, and that listening to their grievances is a waste of time.

The alternative to letting sleeping dogs lie is to risk being bitten. That is to say, for me to speak candidly about the books of certain of my colleagues in the field is to invite their hostility and to wound the feelings of many readers who've enjoyed these books; and this without any expectation of entering on a fruitful dialogue, since I have no confidence at all that we share enough common assumptions about life and literature to enable us to undertake a meaningful discussion. Fan, after all, is a shortened form of fanatic. Moreover, as I've indicated, in many ways I have no quarrel with these books, just as I have no interest in reading them.

Nevertheless I feel that my subject requires me to offer at least one specific instance. Recently I had occasion to read Robert Heinlein's *Starship Troopers*, a book that surely provided Norman Spinrad with one of his models for *The Iron Dream*. Thanks to Norman it isn't necessary to say much concerning

Heinlein's politics. I'm sure that Heinlein himself would reject the label so many of his critics would pin on him, that of 'totalitarian'. He might, after a bit of qualifying, go along with 'authoritarian' since his story does make such an issue of implicit obedience to authority.

What is embarrassing to me about this book is not its politics as such but rather its naïveté, its seeming unawareness of what it is *really* about. Leaving politics aside and turning to that great gushing source of our richest embarrassments, sex, I find *Starship Troopers* to be, in this respect as well, a veritable treasury of unconscious revelations. The hero is a homosexual of a very identifiable breed. By his own self-caressing descriptions one recognises the swaggering leather boy in his most flamboyant form. There is even a skull-and-crossbones earring in his left ear. On four separate occasions when it is hinted in the book that women have sexual attractions, the only such instances in the book, each time within a single page the hero picks a gratuitous fistfight with other servicemen—and he always insists what a lark it is. The association is reflexive and in-variable. Sexual arousal leads to fighting. At the end of the book the hero has become a captain and his father is a sergeant serving under him. This is possible because his mother died in the bombing of Buenos Aires by the Bugs, who are the spiritual doppel-gängers of the human warriors. In an earlier captain-sergeant relation there is a scene, intended to be heart-warming, in which the two men make a date to have a boxing match. Twice the hero makes much of the benefits to be derived from seeing or suffering a lashing. Now all of this taken together is so transparent as to challenge the possibility of its being an unconscious revelation. Yet I'm sure that it was, and that moreover any admirer of the book would insist that it's just my dirty mind that has sullied a fine and patriotic paean to the military life.

So why bring it up at all? For two reasons. The first is that such sexual confusions make the politics of the book more dangerous by infusing them with the energies of repressed sexual desires. It may be that what turns you on isn't the life of an infantryman, but his uniform. A friend of mind has assured me he knew several enlistments directly inspired by a reading of *Starship Troopers*. How much simpler it would have been for those lads just to go and have their ears pierced. The second, related reason is that it is a central purpose of art, in conjunction with criticism, to expand the realm of conscious choice and enlarge the domain of the ego. It does this by making manifest what was latent, a process that can be resisted, but not easily reversed. And so even those who dislike what I have had to say may yet find it useful as a warning of how things appear to other eyes, and be spared, in consequence, needless embarrassment.

At the beginning of this speech I posed the question whether the faults of SF are extraneous to its nature or intrinsic. In looking back at what I've said, my answer would seem to be that they are intrinsic; but then so are its characteristic strengths. SF deals with the largest themes and most powerful emotional materials—but in ways that are often irresponsible and trivialising. Altogether too many of us, even the true giants like Philip Dick, are willing to trust our powers of improvisation untempered by powers of retrospect and analysis. We accept the interest paid to the over-riding fascination of our subject matter as a tribute paid to our talents, which in few cases have been exercised to anything like their full extent. It would be gratifying to add, by way of rounding this off on a mellow note, that none of this much matters—that lousy books don't survive and good books do. And why not, after all, end on that note? It may not be entirely true, but it must be an article of faith for anyone who wants to write good books. I believe it. So should you.

9

Science Fiction: The Monsters and the Critics

PETER NICHOLLS

Originally I had intended to take advantage of my position as organiser and chairman of this lecture series to speak last. I was going to sum up, in a sober and objective way, the various themes that had emerged from the lectures of the nine earlier speakers. The first problem that arose was that I had to give the last position to somebody else. The second problem was that the themes that have emerged are so various that they have thrown my mind into an intellectual ferment.

The metaphorical alcohol this fermentation is producing has persuaded me to take on quite a different rôle, that of amateur exorcist. I imagine myself to be confronted with the body of science fiction. It is strapped to a bed, uttering hoarse, obscene cries, clearly possessed by demons, while its mother and auntie look on helplessly. These two respectable ladies, Mrs Myth and her younger sister, affectionately known as Auntie Fantasy, cannot understand why the child, well brought up and known for his candour and innocence, should so unexpectedly have taken to levitation, the vomiting of filth, the babbling of idiocies, and all the other phenomena so familiar to myself, the exorcist.

I am able to tell the good ladies at once that we are confronted with a case which it will take all my power to cure, a case of multiple possession. An experienced glance tells me that the poor creature is afflicted by demons of two sorts, and borrowing my terminology from a colleague, who by coincidence is one of Auntie Fantasy's close relatives, Professor J. R. R. Tolkien of Oxford University, I name out loud the two families to which the demons belong: they are the monsters and the critics.

In 1936, J. R. R. Tolkien, then known only as a rather obscure Oxford don who specialised in Middle English and Anglo-Saxon, delivered a lecture to the British Academy. The lecture was entitled "Beowulf: The Monsters and The Critics". Tolkien's theme was that the poem *Beowulf* asserted the defiant will of humanity and goodness against overwhelming odds and the forces of darkness. The special pathos, Tolkien believed, was the assertion of this hope in a helpless cause. I like Tolkien's title. It is perfectly apt for my purposes. But the struggle between the doomed forces of light and the inevitably encroaching darkness is not so clear-cut in the case of science fiction as in the case of *Beowulf*.

During its brief and stormy career, science fiction has faced destructive forces of two kinds, those from without and the self-engendered forces from within. I have chosen to call the outside agents of evil 'the critics', and the inside agents 'the monsters'. I will speak most of the time as if all critics are distinct from all monsters. (In fact this is not true. Many a critic is capable, like the werewolf, of instantly becoming a slavering monster himself at the merest glimpse of the full moon.)

In order to proceed with the exorcism, it is necessary to call forth the demons by their rightful names. We'll begin with the critics.

The first group of critics, The Bandwagon Riders, consists usually of people who are not very interested in what they are criticising, and are usually very ignorant about it. Some of them have hoped to make a quiet killing in the American high-school text-book market. Many of them are academics who recognise a comfortable bandwagon when they see one, and genuflect genially towards it before going on, as academics always have done, with whatever interested them in the first place. Such is the reported teacher who takes a university course entitled 'science fiction', and having suckered the enthusiastic students, devotes all his lectures to an analysis of the works of Jonathan Swift.

More dangerous than these harmless parasites are The Conservatives, embittered ignoramuses who detest science fiction without knowing anything about it, imagining it to be a threat to cultural standards, literacy, and the British way of life. They have usually seen a couple of episodes of *Star Trek*, and maybe the second half of *Godzilla meets King Kong* on the late-night television, and may have dim memories of Flash Gordon and Buck Rogers comic strips. They usually attack science fiction for its vulgarity, and if it is tentatively put to them that there is something to be said for H. G. Wells or Aldous Huxley, they simply snort, and say that Wells and Huxley didn't write SF. I think it was Kingsley Amis who put this insight into epigrammatic form:

SF's no good they bellow till we're deaf,
And if it's good, why then it's not SF.

Science fiction has always been very susceptible to this sort of attack. At its worst it is only semi-literate; its rough and raffish demeanour in the early days was reinforced by the lurid illustrations and advertisements for acne cures which used to accompany the stories in the SF magazines. I am quite sure that it was the critics, ignorantly supposing these parts to represent the whole, who delayed the middle-class acceptance of SF until the last decade, even though its energies had been flowing unimpeded for 30 years previously. I had supposed that his particular sort of intellectual snobbery was dead, but no.

I was recently invited to speak on the BBC programme *Start The Week*, to say a few words about science fiction in the context of the ICA lecture series which was then just beginning. In the event I was only given 60 seconds to speak, since the first eight minutes on the subject were taken up by the BBC pundit Kenneth Robinson, who, after the obligatory confession of ignorance at the beginning (much in the manner of Dr Jonathan Miller on a previous BBC occasion) launched himself into an attack on science fiction, on the grounds of its poor writing, which he illustrated with a quote—truly awful indeed—from a story in *Science Fiction Monthly*. (This story, as Mr Robinson did *not* inform the listeners, was written by an amateur for a contest, and not—as he implied—by one of the well-known professionals.) His second ground for dismissing science fiction was that this very lecture series was to be held at the Institute of Contemporary Arts. It seems that Mr Robinson had once visited the Institute of Contemporary Arts ten years ago, and had seen an exhibition which involved a dead horse, a banana, and grass pasted to the walls. From this he concluded that the ICA existed purely to promote pretentious 'high camp', which science fiction must therefore be.

This sort of uninformed and annoying criticism from outside has fostered in science fiction a ghetto mentality, and it is in The Ghetto Critics drawn from the ranks of the fans and the writers that we get this mentality showing most clearly. There is now quite a large body of writing dealing with science fiction, but not yet, I believe, one really good book. What has gone wrong? Inside the walls of the ghetto, all is sociable and chummy. It is often announced in the privacy of fanzines and conventions that science fiction is not subject to the same critical standards as other kinds of literature. Such critics, with the wave of a magic wand, can thus dismiss all criticism by outsiders, who they say are ignorant of the special criteria by which science fiction alone can be judged. However, careful reading of the critical works of, say, Samuel Moskowitz or Donald Wollheim would not reveal what these special criteria might be. All we find is an air of cosy self-congratulation, and an extravagant fannish enthusiasm for the second rate, going together with an extraordinary mistrust of anything that could be labelled—in inverted commas—'intellectual'. The list of writers Wollheim does not mention at all in his study of science fiction, *The Universe Makers*, is quite remarkable. It includes Alfred Bester, James Blish, Philip K. Dick, Thomas M. Disch, Ursula Le Guin, Charles Harness, Frank Herbert, Henry Kuttner, Walter Miller and William Tenn. He makes up for these omissions by waxing eloquent about Edgar Rice Burroughs, André Norton and A. Bertram Chandler. The sort of ghetto criticism represented by Wollheim and Moskowitz must have played its part, though a small one, in making science fiction look ridiculous. With friends like these, who needs enemies?

More sophisticated and influential, and perhaps ultimately more wounding to the genre they profess to love, are The Elegant Slummers, a group of critics best represented by Kingsley Amis and Robert Conquest, who between them edited, for some years, a series of science fiction anthologies called *Spectrum*.

Amis and Conquest, I suspect, came to science fiction as most of us do, in adolescence, at which time the mixture of novelty and fast-paced narrative is what most attracts. Highly sophisticated men, knowing to the point of cynicism in other respects, they appear to see in science fiction a little patch of nostalgic innocence, where everything is simpler and more clear cut. In adulthood, just like roistering bravos from the court seeking out a jolly pub with buxom bar maids at the poor end of town, they enjoy slumming it. But everything is spoiled for the experienced slummer if he becomes a leader of fashion. That marvellous little East End pub, where in the good old days you could buy well-known gangsters a drink, loses its primitive charm and gusto as soon as it gets mentioned in the gossip columns. The next time you visit it you are just as likely to meet Lord Snowdon or Bernard Levin there. Just such a relationship as this is the one I diagnose between Amis and Conquest on the one hand, and science fiction on the other. Science fiction has been spoiled for them by its ever increasing popularity with others of their class: hence the querulous harkings back to the good old days, the anthologies consisting almost entirely of stories from *Astounding*, and the often-repeated contempt for so-called New Wave writing. Amis's criticism, especially in his book, *New Maps of Hell*, is in many ways excellent. Within the narrow confines of the restricted sort of science fiction he is examining, his judgements are difficult to fault. He rightly singles out, for example, Kornbluth & Pohl, Robert Sheckley, Philip K. Dick and Alfred Bester for special praise. But there is no real seriousness in the criticism. He is, for one thing, not nearly as harsh as he ought to have been with other writers. He carelessly loves them all, and feels a little ashamed of himself for doing so. (One feels an emptiness behind it all, as one does in the case of the true promiscuous rake.) It would be an error in good taste, Amis seems to imply, to import real critical values from the great world outside into the jolly noisy slums of SF with their scarlet light glimmering through the polluted fog.

Even Brian Aldiss, a more distinguished critic in many ways, seems to suffer from the same nostalgia, confessing with the printed equivalent of a sheepish smile how he is still enraptured with the old Frank R. Paul covers, the space operas, the sheer monstrous absurdity and energy of the good old days. It's hard not to feel sympathy with this. I feel it strongly myself. One of my favourite anthologies of science fiction is *The Astounding–Analog Reader* edited by Brian Aldiss and Harry

Harrison, a veritable gold mine of magnificently silly stories which brings the past so vividly to the inward eye, with all its adolescent longings and adolescent innocence, that a tear begins to roll, with suspicious readiness, down my once smooth cheek.

But I haven't stuck with science fiction all these years still wanting from it exactly what I required when I was sixteen. Nor has Brian Aldiss as his own science fiction, constantly experimental, clearly shows. His most recently-published novel was called *The Eighty-Minute Hour* and sub-titled *A Space Opera*. In a sense it is as much a work of criticism as a novel in its own right, for it parodies the whole gamut of traditional SF absurdities. Where it fails is in its fundamental uncertainty of tone—almost as if it showed a kind of schizophrenia. The affection for the genre is constantly touched by contempt, even malice for its excesses and banalities. But the critical rigour this suggests is lost in a forgiving laugh which occasionally degenerates to an in-group giggle. The novel is far too long for a straight parody, yet we cannot suspend our disbelief and enjoy the story for its own sake, because Aldiss himself forbids us to take it seriously. This paradoxical impulse, to chastise the body of the loved one—in this case SF—and then afterwards to kiss it better and say we didn't mean it, is very commonly met with in the upper strata of science fiction sophistication. To change the metaphor yet again, it is like punishing a child for showing off to the visitors, and yet giggling yourself at his infantile antics. We do the child no good by our indulgence, natural though it is. He ends up by becoming spoiled and vain, and never truly grows up.

Aldiss's criticism of science fiction is by no means restricted to parody and burlesque. He has been writing occasional critical essays on the subject for many years now. This activity recently culminated in a full-scale book, *Billion Year Spree: The History of Science Fiction*, which for all its faults is by a long way the best full-length study of science fiction yet written. I confess the injustice of encapsulating two years of another man's work in a condescending paragraph, so my passing remarks must be taken as referring to only one aspect of the work. Even in this long and careful study, my impression is of a jolliness and heartiness that comes across too strongly. There is not enough stringency and rigour. My own belief is that we can never truly value the good, unless we can compare it with the less than good. *Billion Year Spree* suffers from too promiscuous a benevolence, particularly in the chapters dealing with the period since 1940. Aldiss is a critic with a particularly sensitive ear for language, and an acute eye for imagery, yet somehow—perhaps in the interests of missionary work, and doing a good public-relations job for the genre he loves—the keenness of his senses is put to work only intermittently. The result is that something of the elegant slummer syndrome persists paradoxically even here, in a writer who is native to the region he describes. To return to the insanitary slums of science fiction is for Aldiss (though not for Amis and Conquest) to go home, as he would proudly admit.

Most of the critics mentioned so far, and many others too, also belong to the over-lapping group, The Genealogists, who love to describe science fiction in terms of its parents. The first eight chapters of Aldiss's *Billion Year Spree*—three-quarters of the book—take the story up to the middle 'thirties. The following 40 years, during which 95 per cent of all readable science fiction has been written, are dismissed in three chapters. Moskowitz does the same. So does Bailey in his study *Pilgrims Through Space and Time*. The author Mark Adlard, himself obsessed with the history of science fiction, keeps on exhorting me, with reference to a book I am writing about SF, 'Don't forget the Edwardians!' The spending of such a relatively huge proportion of critical and scholarly time on such a relatively small proportion of the field is rather sad. Science fiction has never been more alive than it is today. We damage it, in our attempts to dignify it by embalming it in its own history.

Before getting on to the monsters, I should mention the last and chronologically most recent group of critics, to which I suspect I belong myself. We are The Smart Alecks. Our fault is in our adoption of an élitist tone. We are witty and well read. We take our metaphors from all over, from geology, dress design, traditional literature or relativistic physics. We do not shudder away from the ridiculous comparison, and if we consider that the best way of pointing up Doc Smith's deficiencies as a writer is by comparing his books with Milton's *Paradise Lost*, we do so with the satisfaction of a job well done, and no sense of incongruity. We are notable for an inability to keep away from the subject of Robert Heinlein. We drag him into every SF argument obsessively, forgetful of our mothers' advice that it will never get well if you pick it. There is something self-serving and self-indulgent in our manner. Because, in this country especially, science fiction is still only marginally an academic subject, we feel free to mix our fundamentally academic observations with an ironic raciness of manner. It must be assumed that academic readers dislike us for our vulgarity, while ordinary readers dislike us for our constant display of our own cleverness. Ultimately we don't do much damage to the genre, but I doubt if we do it much good either —not as much good as we would do by making the same observations in a level, friendly tone, veering neither towards condescension on the one hand nor obscurantism on the other. *New Worlds* magazine in its present pocket-book format has two of the most notable offenders in the field, apart from myself. They are M. John Harrison and John Clute. A typical M. John Harrison critique might be entitled "To The Stars and Beyond on the Fabulous Anti-Syntax Drive". A recent Clute piece, on the same *Eighty-Minute Hour* by Brian Aldiss that I mentioned before, is titled—almost unbelievably—"I say begone! Apotropaic Narcosis, I'm going to Read the Damned Thing, Ha Ha". The article itself is basically intelligent and sensible, but so élitist is its tone, and so ill-judged in the context of the remarks the critic makes about Aldiss being wordy and pretentious, that the mind reels back in dismay, at this truly awe-inspiring piece of critical self-indulgence. Listen to this:

> But to try to shift this rhetoric of communion into the matrix of a book's voice (as in *The Eighty-Minute Hour,* for instance, or in *Nova*) simply and fundamentally cannot succeed, for a book is not a session, nor does its implied author genuinely communicate with hypostasised fans because he (the shape of the implied Aldiss) precisely is the text itself (as we've already claimed), all else being ventriloquism. Having dreamed the incompossible fan, the implied Aldiss (like Theodore Sturgeon and Robert A. Heinlein and Samuel R. Delany) must take responsibility for any gaffes engendered by that false relation; authorship as an oration to fans confuses composition with performance, and creates

that rhetoric of connivance with which the reader (a real fan say) may well be complicit, because it seems flattering, but which ultimately grates the teeth.

(John Clute very decently approached me after the lecture, and asked that if I was also going to use his piece in the book, would I mind printing what he originally wrote, putting some minor misprints from the *New Worlds* version right. I have done so, from his original manuscript.) To whom is John Clute speaking when he writes this? To maybe ten of us, and we get pretty irritated with it.

By naming The Smart Alecks I have finished my roll-call of the critic demons who possess the body of science fiction, in an act of premature necrophilia, for it is not yet quite dead.

I'll drop the exorcism metaphor for the moment, in order to summarise. There are not yet many critics of science fiction and not many of these have really helped the common reader to understand science fiction better, or to see its importance. SF criticism tends to extremes: it is over-dismissive or over-friendly. The criticism so far in print must surely tend to polarise the potential readership of science fiction, serving to reinforce already existing prejudices for it or against it. The unconverted reader who comes across most pro-science-fiction criticism will usually be made to feel left out, lacking the open-sesame to what must seem to him a closed world. (The difficulty for the critic is that if he concentrates his address towards the non-converted general reader, as Brian Ash does in his recent study, *Faces of the Future*, he is apt to seem rather patronising and over-simplifying to the already converted. He is also apt to spend far too much time recounting the details of a great many tortuous plot developments. This difficulty of not knowing precisely who the reader is obviously affected Brian Aldiss too, in *Billion Year Spree*, where he sometimes spells things out rather embarrassingly, as in his reference to Voltaire, 'a French philosopher who wrote over ten million words'.)

Perhaps the basic problem is that critics of science fiction so regularly fall into the habit of speaking of it as if it were a *totally* separate genre, in its own definable pigeon-hole—though the many definitions offered have been notoriously clumsy and unsatisfactory. Perhaps if we were all more ready to admit the continuity between traditional literature and science fiction, then the polarisation of readers into pro- and anti-SF factions would be less marked. The critical distinction important to me, between good and bad books, science fiction or otherwise, is eschewed by most SF critics, who are often leery of value judgements, fearing that the necessary criteria are too obscure and subjective—fearing also, presumably, the accusation of arrogance that can so easily be flung at the evaluative critic.

The risk of being thought arrogant is real, but worth taking. The alternative leaves us with chaos. The new reader is left not knowing where he might profitably begin, faced with the enormous picture gallery of bright SF covers in any large bookshop. His only criteria are those of continuing popularity, so that Asimov, Heinlein, van Vogt, and even Doc Smith, continue to succeed as 'classics' through a kind of inertia—the 'classic' label has an almost irresistible momentum. It takes a very long time for new writers to get up a 'selling' momentum of their own, and while the critics opt out, the field is left free for the often cynical conservatism of book publishers, who, naturally enough, continue to push the books which have been 'good things' in the past. Asimov and Heinlein continue to get the lion's share of the display space. Critics can't change this situation over-night, but at the moment, too few of them even try. This is a field where many critics are as conservative as the publishers, and as content to accept a hierarchy of SF writers which has long since ceased to make sense, if it ever did.

The critics who possess the body of science fiction are irritants at worst. The monsters create the worst wounds—wounds all the more dangerous, in some cases, for being so seldom diagnosed. The monsters are engendered from within science fiction itself; the wounds they inflict are self-inflicted. I can pass quickly over many of them, because previous speakers in this lecture series have described them. Ursula Le Guin spoke eloquently of the Monster of Flat Characterisation and Inhumanity. You will recall her saying that science fiction would only be healthy so long as it made room for Mrs Brown. John Brunner fought like a veritable St George against the Dragon-Monster of Pseudo Science. Harry Harrison casually aimed a bludgeon blow at the crafty beast whose name is Selling-Your-Soul-To-Commerce (though this passage does not appear in the version of his lecture revised for print). Tom Disch used the iron fist in the velvet glove as he quietly took a strange-hold on the Hydra-Headed Monster he named The Embarrassments of Science Fiction. You will remember that each of the heads had a different name. There was Power Fantasy, Elitism for the Unsuccessful Technocrat, Sublimated Sexuality and Infantilism.

It seems that half of the exorcism has been completed for me, and my job is just to mop up. Some of the more subtle monsters I wish to name, however, though deceptively small and meek in appearance, have mean and devious natures. Each of them constitutes a genuine threat.

Before describing my first monster, The Sentimental Stylist, I need to give you some background. In the early 1950s, when I began reading science fiction, there was very little criticism available. Most of what I could find was in the form of newspaper reviews, or review columns in the SF magazines. It became clear that even those who most loved science fiction tended to feel edgy and embarrassed at its stilted prose, a sort of second-hand derivation of the journalistic workmanlike style of contemporary thrillers and detective stories. It was generally agreed that Isaac Asimov and Robert Heinlein, for example, were a good step up from Doc Smith as word-smiths, but there was a way to go yet. Everyone seemed to be waiting for a true science fiction stylist, and two of them came along. They were Ray Bradbury and Theodore Sturgeon.

When I was first reading science fiction, Ray Bradbury was the name on everybody's lips. In Australia at least, if anyone said he had read only one book of science fiction, you could pretty well bet in advance that it was either a Ray Bradbury or a John Wyndham. Bradbury was greeted with delight, because of his style, generally accepted as poetic and sensitive. In no time at all he graduated from the SF magazines to the *Saturday Evening Post*, where he found his niche. I'd like to suggest that the *Saturday Evening Post* was *exactly* the right niche for Bradbury. The unexceptionable cosiness and sentimentality with which over many decades, the *Saturday Evening Post* reassured readers that the fundamental decencies of the American way of life still had their staunch adherents, corresponded precisely to the values of life which Bradbury himself espoused. In classic Bradbury story after story, the down-home sentiment of the small mid-western township (which in the real world had almost ceased to exist) triumphed against unfeeling technology. Bradbury touched a chord which reverberated, it seems, throughout the hearts of America, especially the heartland hearts. The sentiments he espoused were indeed *decent*. My quarrel with them is that they were also soft, and unreal. People accepted them so readily because they could do so comfortably, without having to think.

There was a curious underside to all of this, which revealed itself progressively over the years. Along with the small-town Utopian sentiments went something, it seems to me, of the small-town prurience and prudish obsession with the dark side of things. More and more Bradbury stories came to be set in October, the month of Halloween. His images lost the smell of lilac, and the scent of sarsaparilla, and began to take on the damp earthy smell of the freshly-dug grave. Boneless creatures, self-mutilators, hysterics, began to appear at the focus of his stories; and more and more, it seems to me, he began to wallow in those feelings which he affected to despise.

Something of all this is reflected in what I find to be the fairly obvious falseness of his style. Too often it was a poetry of whimsy and cuteness. It lacked hard lines—it settled for the vague evocation rather than the specific re-creation. Let me read you a much-praised passage from Bradbury's most-praised novel, known here as *The Silver Locusts*, and published in 1951:

... the men shuffled forward, only a few at first, a double-score, for most men felt the great illness in them even before the rocket fired into space. And this disease was called The Loneliness, because when you saw your home town dwindle to the size of your fist, and then lemon-size and then pin-size and vanish in the fire-wake, you felt you had never been born, there was no town, you were nowhere, with space all around, nothing familiar, only other strange men. And when the state of Illinois, Iowa, Missouri or Montana vanished into cloud seas, and, doubly, when the United States shrank to a misted island and the entire planet Earth became a muddy baseball tossed away, then you were alone, wandering in the meadows of space, on your way to a place you couldn't imagine.

This is insidious bad writing, of the kind that is often taken as very good writing indeed. I notice that the incantatory repetitive rhythms lull the reader away from the actual meaning. The images are chosen for their nostalgia content rather than their aptness: the lemon-sized town, the muddy baseball tossed away, and worst of all, 'wandering in the meadows of space'. It is totally unreal. I don't believe for a minute that a pig-farmer from Iowa would think of himself, crammed into a rocket with a crowd of strangers, with stomach churning, as 'wandering in the meadows of space'. Bradbury puts it that way to evoke from us all the stock responses that 'wandering in meadows' has given to us ever since the myth of Proserpine or before, and to hell with its relevance.

I focus on Bradbury rather than Sturgeon, because he is more widely known outside the field, though inside the field, I suspect, it was Sturgeon who found greater favour. Sturgeon was a good writer much of the time. It's a pity he was praised so much, so prematurely, for there's a great laziness in his writing, too. It reverts obsessively to the same themes, which ultimately are pretty woman's-magaziney. He is very strong on the redemptive power of love, for instance. And like Bradbury, he has rather a glutinous obsession with death, mutilation, the cruelty of children. I recommend the story "The Professor's Teddy Bear" to you. (You can find it in the collection *E Pluribus Unicorn*.) It is extraordinarily incoherent in its desperate flaying about with the images of blood, sex, childhood and corruption, and reads like one long-drawn-out schizophrenic scream. The combination of superficial 'fine' writing with a comfortable sentimentality, overlaying a kind of leprous fear-imagery, is quite common in literature generally, and in science fiction in particular.

The danger of making too many critical points in a brief lecture is over-statement, without even the proper time to make out a complete case. Bradbury and Sturgeon are by no means alone. There are others in the same sort of category—Roger Zelazny and Harlan Ellison for example; perhaps even that great favourite of the SF *literati*, Cordwainer Smith, whose undoubted elegance always seems a touch old-fashioned and rather coy to me, showing something of the self-indulgence and mild decadence of a Ronald Firbank.

My quarrel is not with the writers themselves. They have all given me much pleasure at various times. Bradbury's short story "In a Season of Calm Weather"—the one about the Picasso fan who meets his idol drawing pictures in the sand—is unforgettable. Sturgeon's "Killdozer" and *More Than Human* will rightly be remembered for a long time. Zelazny's *This Immortal* is a strong novel. I recall Ellison's "Pretty Maggie Moneyeyes" with great pleasure.

My quarrel is with the self-consciousness of a field which praises too highly and too prematurely the work of self-conscious literary stylists—encouraging self-indulgence with their un-abashed admiration and cosy fannish bonhomie. This kind of praise is self-enclosed, and seemingly unaware of what standards of excellence are to be found in the world of fiction outside the field of science fiction, where Bradbury and Sturgeon might easily be judged as no more than skilful commercial writers, deploying a conventional armoury of conventional sentiments in order to evoke conventional reactions.

More to the point, even within science fiction, there was genuine originality of a different kind going on elsewhere. James Blish at his best, for example, was a harder and more intelligent writer than Sturgeon, though not free of senti-mentality himself. While Sturgeon was writing we were also able to read stories by Alfred Bester, Kornbluth & Pohl, Robert Sheckley, even the early J. G. Ballard—all of them, surely, finer and more original than Sturgeon. Bester especially never had the praise he deserved from his contemporaries, in my view, although he did win the first Hugo in 1953 with *The Demolished Man*.

The conjunction of Ellison, Zelazny, Bradbury, Sturgeon and Cordwainer Smith, incidentally, brings up several other associated monstrosities. I have encapsulated the flimsier aspects of their work as 'sentimental stylist', but they could also be called 'anti-science', or even 'fantasy-masquerading-as-science-fiction'. Any of these titles would fit any of the five writers named, and some others as well, whom I didn't include in my first list because they have not received the same degree of over-ripe praise. They would include Philip José Farmer, Clifford Simak, Anne McCaffrey, and even Fritz Leiber—although Leiber, for all his irritating obsession with cats and Shakespeare, and his self-conscious colloquial gusto, has written some fine stories, not easy to categorise.

I don't intend dwelling on the fact which most baffles outsiders coming to science fiction—the fact that so many of its most revered names have an inability to comprehend either the workings or effects of science and technology, which often emerges as a contemptuous disregard for plausibility. This is a familiar paradox in the field, and is the fault of the early publicists who landed us with the phrase 'science fiction', which has never been especially appropriate. The writers can hardly be blamed for the label pinned on them, even though that label continues to arouse expectations in the naïve which are seldom fulfilled.

I won't dwell on subsequent monsters to the same degree as I have with the sentimental stylist. I regard the sentimental stylists as especially damaging because (through no fault of their own) they have landed the younger readers of science fiction—and most readers of science fiction *are* younger—with a warped and inadequate sense of what literary style might be—something verbose and flowery and constantly hovering on the brink of easy sentiment. The presence of feeling in a story, it can't be repeated too often, is no guarantee of quality. Everything depends on the accuracy with which the feeling is rendered, and its aptness to its object.

Next we confront a grinning gargoyle, too tiny for us to say with confidence that he is either a monster or a critic. He is The Blurb Writer. I will give you just one example, a notably typical blend of inaccuracy, inadequate syntax, over-statement, and the worst kind of chauvinism. The novel is *Sign of the Labrys* by Margaret St Clair, a very stylish and lively fantasy which deserves to be better known. Miss St Clair is done no favour by the back cover of the Corgi edition, which reads:

WOMEN ARE WRITING SCIENCE FICTION. ORIGINAL! BRILLIANT! DAZZLING! Women are closer to the primitive than men. They are conscious of the moon-pulls, the earth-tides. They possess a buried memory of humankind's obscure and ancient past which can emerge to uniquely color and flavor a novel.

Such a woman is Margaret St Clair. . . .

and so on for several more lines. It is interesting how many men rationalise their instinctive chauvinistic belief that women are dangerous alien creatures by imputing supernatural powers to them and creating bitch goddesses. (This seizing on an apparently objective pseudo-truth allows men to turn away from their own feelings of guilt about women.)

The next monster is a paradoxical creature, because he doesn't look like a monster at all—he doesn't look nearly as much like a monster as he should. He is the Insufficiently Monstrous Alien. My favourite example is from Hal Clement's *Mission of Gravity*, in which we find the society of Mesklinites. They are so different from us in appearance and environment as to be awe-inspiring until they open their mouths, whereupon they sound exactly like Calvin Coolidge. The Insufficiently Monstrous Alien is first cousin to his more alarming fellow anthropomorph, The Insufficiently Alien Society. It is truly amazing how often, especially in those two grand old men of SF, Isaac Asimov and Robert Heinlein, galactic society turns out to operate almost entirely under the discredited mode of *laissez-faire* capitalism and free trade which ceased even to work in our own society some time in the late 'twenties. I enjoy Asimov's "Foundation" trilogy as much as the next man, in terms of what will happen next. The carefully delayed resolution of the mystery—Where is the Second Foundation?—makes the book an entertaining thriller. But it is almost incredible to me that these three books are taken by many, possibly including Asimov himself, as serious statements about the nature of historical evolution. This despite the fact that the galaxy is saved by a precocious fourteen-year-old girl called Arkady. Yep, there's a real sophisticated historical thesis in there. Incidentally, Asimov's *End of Eternity* argues the case against social engineering far more convincingly than the "Foundation" trilogy argues the case for it.

Anthropomorphism in science fiction is a very difficult monster to overcome. We are bound to interpret the alien in terms we can understand, for otherwise it remains simply blank.

Two science fiction novels—and very fine ones at that—actually take this anthropomorphising habit of humanity, so especially obvious in Heinlein, Asimov and Clement, as their subject matter. I recommend anyone interested in the subject to read Algis Budrys's *Rogue Moon* and Stanislaw Lem's *Solaris*.

Moving rapidly through the remaining monsters, I come next to the Monster of Anarchy. This one is very interesting indeed, and he deserves a long and careful study to be made of him. (The study has since been written: see *Foundation: The Review of Science Fiction* No. 9.) In the meantime I restrict myself to saying that the portrayal of a fragmenting and decaying world whose moral values are totally inadequate to the task of saving it, has produced some of the most compelling science fiction of the last decade. But how do we portray fragmentation? With what voice? From what point of view? Does the portrayal of anarchy and nihilism necessarily require the abdication of all moral judgement in the narrator? My own feeling is that such an abdication can only be achieved by a conscious repudiation of the author's own humanity, because rightly or wrongly we all do judge, we all *do* have preferences about the kinds of life we feel to be good.

I would produce three compelling but in some ways distasteful novels as my prime documents here. They are *Crash* by J. G. Ballard, *Barefoot in the Head* by Brian Aldiss, and *The English Assassin* by Michael Moorcock—the finest so far in his as-yet-uncompleted Jerry Cornelius tetralogy. All these books are different in tone, but they have some features in common. The first is a very heavy emphasis on things—objects and places, clothes, cars, advertisements, guns, records, together with a diminishment of focus on character. It is as if character were coming to be seen as definable only in terms of environment and life style. All three books are notably cool and unimpassioned: *Crash* is the most extreme, and *Barefoot in the Head* the least so, although Aldiss's greater readiness to admit human passions is partly defused by the ornate and baroque prose with which he creates them. Moorcock and Ballard both write coolly and sparely. Indeed, the Monster of Anarchy is characterised above all by his cool. He saunters laconically through landscapes pitted and scarred by the stigmata of self-destruction, resting occasionally in the Garden of

Gethsemane, asking and expecting no advice or assistance from any quarter, human or godly. He fucks a lot, and does so most cheerfully when surrounded by the detritus of destruction, the crashed car, the dully gleaming carbine slung over the shoulder, the empty syringe lying on the toilet floor. This Monster worries me, not least because it may be he is not so much a product of literature as of life itself. I am not yet personally prepared to admit or welcome his over-riding presence, and I am not happy about those writers who do, although I know (and this is what makes the case so worrying) that the writers who seem to welcome his presence include some of the finest working in our field.

I was going to talk about the Monster of Unfulfilled Promise. But though a melancholy creature, he always offers the hope that one day, as in the transformation scene of Beauty and the Beast, he may appear most handsomely as a prince. Much sadder is my final monster, the Monster of Fulfilled Promise.

It has been said that every writer has one obsessive theme to which he constantly returns. This is even more true inside science fiction than out of it. It very often happens in SF that the archetypal story by which a writer is remembered came very early or even first in his career. There are obvious exceptions—the writers who started very moderately, often churning out material for the pulps, and then slowly matured. Robert Silverberg and John Brunner are two writers whose recent work is notably in a different class from their earlier copious efforts. A less prolific younger writer showing every sign of maturing is Christopher Priest. We need expend no pity on the writer who continues to improve.

No, the Monster of Fulfilled Promise is found with those writers who continue, with variations, to write their first books over and over again. Sometimes, as with Alfred Bester and Walter Miller, perhaps in recognition of the danger of repeating themselves, they retire early from the field. More commonly, they continue. Think of Cyril Kornbluth, Poul Anderson, Arthur Clarke, A. E. van Vogt, Theodore Sturgeon, John Christopher, John Wyndham, Robert Heinlein, Clifford Simak, Larry Niven, Frederik Pohl, Frank Herbert, Roger Zelazny, Eric Frank Russell. The list is by no means complete, but in every case I think it's fair to say that the writer set the pattern

with one or more of his first few books, and then cleaved to the
pattern ever after. Some of them were never very good. Others
were very good indeed. But they fulfilled their promise, and we
await their new books—I do at least—with a slight sense of
dreariness, and a strong sense of incipient *déjà vu.*

We must blame ourselves for this. One of the basic paradoxes
of science fiction, usually thought to be the literature of
conceptual exploration, is that it contains within it very strong
commercial pressures to do more of the same. I noticed that
after Harry Harrison spoke in this series, four or five of the
audience came up and asked him when we could expect another
Deathworld book. I'd like another Deathworld book myself,
and I'm no more free of blame than any of us, but this sort of
rigid conservatism, multiplied by all the millions of readers,
may yet be the kiss of death for the entire genre. We suffocate it
with our love, our desire that it should stay forever young and
beautiful. We want the same novelties, over and over again.
A *novel* novelty requires from us an act of will and intelligence
to enjoy it. We cry out for originality, then look at it with
vague distaste when it arrives, as when our wives cut their hair
or change the colour of their lipstick. Conservative Expectation
is one of the most notable monsters, and is created neither by
the writers nor the critics, though both conspire in its birth. It
comes ultimately from *us*, the readers.

Well here am I, the exorcist, and here are you, the audience.
All of us are gazing bemused at the tattered and pustular body
of science fiction lying before us, tied to its bed. We see it being
sucked slowly into the shapeless, amoeboid body of that great
vicious protozoan blob whose name is Mainstream. We see it
bleeding from the jagged wounds left by the critics who,
snarling, drag away lumps of flesh dripping a foetid ichor, or
else smother it with loathsome incestuous kisses. We see it
feverish from the inner ulcerations, anaemias and cancers set
up by its own numerous antibodies, the monsters. Science fiction
cannot maintain the integrity of its fragmenting body; it rejects
its own proteins; it sloughs off the healing grafts it is offered.

What can we feel, gazing at all of this? Compassion, perhaps;
nausea, almost certainly. Would it not be kindest to have this
sick, mutilated creature put down? Or should we simply wait
for the merciful release of entropy, which will ultimately

scatter its decaying atoms to the eight corners of the universe? (I have always envisaged the universe as a very big, black cube.)

And what are we to make of the 200-odd members of the ICA audience, returning week after week? Are we to see you, to see ourselves, as so many emotionally crippled Madame Desfarges, knitting at the foot of the guillotine and listening to the thump of each successive head? Are you, perhaps, sadists, like those whose special pleasure it was in watching hangings to sense the victim's last spasmodic reflex and orgasm as his neck snapped? Could it be that the present apparent vigour of science fiction is no more than this pleasureless jolt?

In fact, this is all nonsense. I don't withdraw anything at all I've said, but I confess I must, somehow, have failed to reach the essence of the matter. Science fiction is *not* a literature for morons. This audience does *not* consist of sixteen-year-old boys, who regularly have sand kicked in their face, asking for more and more Conan and Lensman books. After four years of extremely close professional connection with science fiction (and almost nothing *but* science fiction), I often get impatient. But I still retain a lot of enthusiasm. I'm still forced to admit there must be something in it. The intelligence of the science fiction audience, manifest in this lecture series, in fanzines, in classes, in conversation, even at conventions, must be a response to *something*.

The previous speakers in this series, of course, were not wholly on the attack. Edward de Bono praised science fiction for what he called 'provocation'—the ability to tug the mind into new frames of reference, where apparently insoluble problems begin to make sense. Professor John Taylor sees SF as an inspirational fiction, having the knack and prime virtue of making scientific thoughts interesting. Harry Harrison avers that it gets 'the old brain working', and adds in parenthesis that it is often a literature of freedom, internationalist and classless in scope. Alan Garner sees it as the modern form of myth, holding within it avatars of the ancient and still potent archetypes. Alvin Toffler sees it helping to cushion us against the shocks of the future.

All the critics and monsters I enumerated are real enough threats, but I believe that science fiction is a much tougher beast than we might imagine, and that the praises of the previous speakers are very largely justified.

Part of our problem as Tom Disch pointed out in the previous lecture, is in the very term 'science fiction'. We speak as if it is a definable, self-consistent unitary genre. In fact it is not, and never has been. One kind of science fiction, therefore, can be so possessed by monsters as to be pustular and purulent to the point of obscenity, while another kind continues happily on in rude health.

We tend to speak, also, as if SF were different from all other literatures, while the truth is that there is a demonstrable continuity with other literature, both vertically, going back through time, and horizontally, across the spectrum of the different kinds all being written at *this* time. I could do (and have done before) a literary exercise where I demonstrate that there is a mainstream equivalent of almost every great science-fiction theme, but tonight, in my act of exorcism, I want to emphasise some of the differences, to emphasise what qualities we can still find in science fiction which allow it to excite us, despite all the onslaught of monsters and critics combined. The exorcist cannot work on a possessed mind that has lost all concept of godliness, but SF is not yet in hell. Rather, it is slowly clambering upwards through the cleansing flames of purgatory.

Here, to conclude, are some of the reasons I take science fiction to be ultimately healthy, and the reasons why it is important to me.

First, it is the great modern literature of metaphor. Conventional literature has a limit, set by everyday realism, to the juxtapositions of imagery it can allow itself. Science fiction, which can create its own worlds, has access to new juxtapositions. The unexpected and witty conjunction of disparate images has long been recognised to be one of the great strengths of poetry. Science fiction can do it too. I'll give two examples. One is from Brian Aldiss's novel *An Age*, also published under the title of *Cryptozoic*. That novel begins with an artist working on a lonely beach. Soon it becomes clear that it is not a beach of today—that it is the primal red sandstone beach of the Devonian era, set way back in the artist's past. He has come to an age of evolution where the lung fish are flopping from the sea to the land—the great turning point in history to which the artist responds, because it has led to *him*, and it also helps him understand the ancient pull of the salt sea echoed in the constituents of his own blood. Suddenly this peaceful scene is blasted apart, and over the hill arrives (impossibly in this context, in any traditional novel) a gang of leather boys. This is an extraordinarily moving and violent poetry of contrast.

The second example is from the leading story in *New Worlds 8*. The story is called "Running Down", and is by that same M. John Harrison I mentioned before as one of the critics. It is a bleak, vivid and elaborate metaphor of entropy, focused in the shabby figure of an unsuccessful accident-prone Cambridge graduate. The images work serially, from a cut-finger, through a prematurely aged and surly woman, and then through her blackened fire-burned body. Moving and strong, the story to this point could almost be mainstream. But its final image, which sums up all the others, could only appear in science fiction. We are moved violently from the world of domestic accident to the world of apocalypse, as the gangling, now almost insane, protagonist climbs a peak in the Lake District, lightning flickering around his head, shouts his cry of pain, and becomes the epicentre of an earthquake which roars its way across the end of the tale. In mainstream terms it is as if we moved from Margaret Drabble to *King Lear* in the space of twenty pages. It could only happen in the science fiction tradition. In no other way could this metaphor of entropy be so satisfyingly complete. Even the end—a mainstream end, so to speak—is stronger from its SF context. It goes like this:

> And I prefer to picture Stickle Tarn not as it looked from the 1,600 foot contour during Lyall's final access of rage and despair, but as I remember it from my Cambridge days and before—a wide, cold pool in the shadow of an ancient and beautiful cliff, where on grey windy days a seabird you can never identify seems always to be trawling twenty feet above the water in search of something it probably can't even define to itself.

The second special strength of SF is related to the first. It is able to incorporate intellectually *shocking* material, partly because it is so pre-eminently the literature of change, as opposed to mainstream literature, which is the literature of human continuity. This has been specially so in recent years; moving away from blandness and whimsy, SF is becoming notably tougher. Tom Disch spoke of irony, and I believe it is the incorporation of the possibilities of irony into traditional science fiction that has given it much of its recent strength. Very much so in Disch's own work, and also in that of Robert Sheckley, the final lecturer in this series. *New Worlds* magazine in England, for all its excesses, repetitions and self-indulgences, pioneered the use of a more adult tone in science fiction. I don't think it is any accident that during the decade in which this took place, a new word—one I've already mentioned—came to be dominant in science fiction. The word is 'entropy' —previously a rather obscure term from the discipline of thermodynamics. In the recent concentration on entropy, in the work of Philip Dick in the USA, and the *New Worlds* writers over here, science fiction found the right metaphor for the times. Great literature has always been focused on the contrast between the evanescence of life, love and passion, and the permanence of death and decay. Science fiction, which up to the 1950s had typically though not inevitably paid little attention to the tragic reverberations of life, thus rendering it all too likely that it would continue only as a literature of infantilism, suddenly found that the scientific idea of the heat death of the universe was the perfect correlative for the Jacobean idea of death, both the little death of the sexual act, and the greater death at the end of life. Where SF once beamed out on to the world with an expression of fatuous trust, quite free of irony in either incident or tone, it developed adulthood with the admission, implicit in the natural randomness of the universe, that things go wrong, decay, surprise, collapse. James Blish, a writer often under-rated these days, was one of the first to recognise this in science fiction.

It is important to see that I'm not just simple-mindedly recommending pessimism over optimism. I am recognising the more subtle double awareness of irony over the single awareness of unsupported hope. The ironist is not a cruel man, but he is ready for the worst as well as the best. His objectivity is necessary to keep the forces of destruction from overwhelming him with sheer feeling, to the exclusion of thought.

Third, science fiction is the literature of the outsider, in the extreme sense. Traditional realist fiction observes its action from the viewpoint of a partaker. It shares the illusions of the society which produces it. So does all fiction, but it is science fiction which makes the conscious effort, sometimes quite successful, to stand outside, to give us the Martian eye view of affairs. In this respect, incidentally, it grows straight out of eighteenth-century satire. Jonathan Swift's voice lives on in Sheckley and Disch. We need this mental tool, which SF offers us, as a way of getting outside ourselves and our societies.

Fourthly, science fiction allows us to escape, but gives us the choice of escaping into a world where all is not easy. It offers us as many hells as heavens, and in this respect its reputation for escapism needs to be modified.

Fifthly, the freedom of imagery available to the science-fiction writer allows him to derive a potency of effect, whether consciously or unconsciously, from his own hopes and fears, which, in the way of archetypes, are likely to be ours too. The collapsing star, the monstrous embrace, the brilliant child misunderstood by his parents, the dying tribe, the animal which is a machine, and the machine that is an animal—these and many other familiar images of science fiction have all the obsessive power of myth. In other words, even the inexperienced SF writer is working with materials that often cut very deep. This is why, in my view, it is pre-eminently the modern literature not of physics, but of metaphysics. It is in science fiction that we are now asking the deepest questions of meaning and causation.

Finally, I admit that my rôle of exorcist is doomed to failure. The simple naming of monsters and critics is not enough to make them go away. All of *us*, and many more, would need to chant the exorcism rites for a long time, before any result was visible. I think we *should* do it. Science fiction is growing up now, and not so much in need of our protection, our embarrassed camouflage of its faults whenever an outsider makes a nasty comment.

Already the monsters are less obvious than they were ten years ago. Science fiction has never been more exciting than it is today. A literature being served by such writers as Ursula Le Guin, Philip Dick, Tom Disch, Harry Harrison, John Brunner, Alan Garner, Robert Sheckley, and our chairman tonight, one of the finest of younger writers, Ian Watson—such a literature has much life left in it. Along with those names, think of the best of Brian Aldiss, J. G. Ballard, Michael Moorcock, Gene Wolfe, and Bob Shaw (who is surely by a long way the most intelligent of all those still writing traditional SF). Think of the best of Richard Cowper, D. G. Compton and Samuel Delany. I mean this to be more than a conventional signing off. By contrast with the science fiction achievements of today, for all of us not blinded by tears of nostalgia, the so-called golden age of the 1940s was an age of Lead.

10

The Search for the Marvellous

ROBERT SHECKLEY

ROBERT SHECKLEY

I have always regarded Robert Sheckley as one of the finest short-story writers in science fiction. I seem to have been enjoying his stories almost from the time I learned to lisp the alphabet. I was amazed to discover that he is only a few years older than myself. What a prodigious adolescence he must have had, inventing extraordinary science fiction societies which are often a monstrous and painfully accurate travesty of the sillier aspects of our own, at a time when most right-thinking youths are preoccupied with trying to borrow their father's car.

I would like to boast that I had planned this good-humoured and enormously successful climax to the lecture series from the beginning, but as Mr Sheckley himself explains below, it was a happy and last-minute accident. Indeed, I had been warned that inviting him to speak was roughly comparable to travelling back in time and, with full knowledge, booking a ticket on the *Titanic*. 'He has a *dreadful* stammer' was the universal cry, but bent on self-destruction, and determined to see fair play done to our inarticulate brothers, I persisted. He was difficult to locate, but by then I was obsessed with getting this prodigy of muteness along, as a symbol of broad-mindedness, in the same spirit as I would like to have invited the late, stone-deaf Beethoven to be a judge of the International Brass Band Championships.

The only way of reaching Robert Sheckley unless you are unwise enough to trust the postal system of the Balearic Isles—I swear this is true—is by placing an international 'phone call to Sandy's Bar in Santa Eulalia. Sandy, who answered the 'phone, reassured me that Mr Sheckley would be in later. His tone of voice made Sheckley sound rather like Ray Milland in *Lost Weekend*.

In the event, my dicing with disaster came out just fine. Never before has a stammer been put to such skilful use. On the page, Mr Sheckley's piece is funny, but unless you can imagine the mode of its delivery, you are unlikely to laugh with quite the same abandon as the audience at the ICA. And, among other things, the fact that this was the final lecture served to remind the audience, who had spent a number of weeks dutifully having deep thoughts, that the most common reason for reading science fiction is that ultimately it is fun.

As a final aid to readers, please note that the serious passages are to be read out in a totally different voice. How Mr Sheckley, with his crippling defects as a speaker, managed this obscure ventriloquial feat, I shall never know.

I was asked about a month ago to substitute for Philip K. Dick, who was supposed to speak to you tonight. I accepted, and sat down to prepare a speech.

I am not an experienced speaker. I am a stammerer. I shy away from speaking before groups of one person or more. I even stammer when talking to myself. But friends told me that a stammer is considered a mark of intelligence in England, and all the best people do it. Thus, my stammer, far from being a drawback, was a positive asset. So it looks as though we're both lucky tonight—me for having a stammer, and you for being privileged to hear it.

I have only spoken before an audience once before—last year at a college in New York, where I substituted for Frank Herbert. And now I am substituting again. I could see that I was beginning a new and promising career as a substitute science fiction writer-speaker—a sort of pinch hitter of the lecture circuits.

But in order for this dream to come true, I needed a speech I could deliver. It couldn't be the one I had done in New York, because I ad libbed that from cards and it was a disaster. Stammering science fiction writers with unclear ideas should avoid ad libbing.

First I thought I would do a lecture about the future. After all, science fiction is all about the future. But I'm not in a good position for that, since in fact I live in the past.

I live on the Spanish island of Ibiza with my wife, my child, two dogs, a cat, and a house guest. I live there in a 200-year-old stone farmhouse built like a fortress. It has seven rooms but only two windows. We have no television, no telephone, no radio. Just a lot of almond trees.

As far as the future is concerned, Ibiza is out of it. If Western civilisation came to a sudden end, we wouldn't know about it until three days later when we read about it in *Time* magazine.

Back when I lived in New York, I always had a lot of ideas about the future. Basically, the future was a grim, crowded, noisy, dangerous place, unstable, illogical, stimulating, and subject to change without notice. Just like home. But now I live on Ibiza, where thing have been going along at pretty much the same pace and style since the landing of the first Roman tourists.

Ibiza lives in an eternal past, and is unafflicted by modern culture. Ibiza, in fact, has no modern culture. It has no culture at all as far as I've been able to make out.

I would like to clarify that remark, however. There are many cultured and intelligent people of all nationalities on the island. But there is no culture because there are no cultural outlets. Certainly not for English speakers, which is all I am a speaker of. There are no movies for us, no rock concerts, no libraries, lectures, theatre, bookstores, and so forth. There are only the sea and the mountains, the flowering fields and the polluted beaches.

Since I am a professional I plugged on, organised my data, and off and on during this time I was thinking, 'What exactly am I supposed to be talking about?' Because I knew if I could figure that out everything would be fine.

I looked at the programme of these lectures to see what the other speakers were up to. As well as I could judge from the titles, they were into some serious stuff. That was all right with me: I can be as serious as the next man.

And, in fact, there was something I wanted to say. I wanted to mention the psychological effects of the downfall of the Ptolemeian man-centred universe. This conception, as I'm sure you all remember, mediated men's ideas about the unknown for many centuries. It was a perfectly symmetrical scheme, and it strangled speculation.

But now we live in an entirely different conceptual place. In our present orientation we are inhabitants of one planet circling a minor star in an uninteresting suburb of a medium-sized galaxy in one among many island-universes.

Science has brought us to this, and has freed us to face the inevitable probability of other existences, other lives not necessarily related to or derived from us.

Science has brought us to the threshold of actual participation in the unknown. But that's as far as most of us will ever go. For most of us are participants in science only as consumers and spectators. We watch their accomplishments on television, and buy the fruits of their investigations in the form of television sets and automobiles.

When the first man sets foot on the surface of Mars, we will participate only to the extent of watching a shadowy replay of the great event on television. You know already how it will go: announcers with sonorous voices will tell us exactly what is happening. And they will also cue us as to the proper emotions we should feel at every stage of the great adventure. That will be our share in the conquest of other worlds.

The scientists' motives may be pure, but their pretensions are sometimes hard to take. They want to explore the unknown for us and report back their findings—as if the rest of us weren't equally explorers, moving between the mysteries of life and death just as they do.

At present, members of one particular group possess the exclusive means of transport; the equipment, the hardware required for contact with other worlds. We, the people, subsidise this work, but the manufacturers and the military reap the immediate benefit. For us is reserved the entertainment value.

The scientist, who examines everything, should look at himself. Tentatively I would define him as a discovery-producing animal whose products fall from him as naturally and as thoughtlessly as a hen produces eggs. Like the hen, he is largely indifferent to the use made of his products. Scientists are mostly not in favour of atom bombs, of course, and hens presumably dislike omelettes; but both are realists and go along with the conditions they find.

The trouble is, science is oriented towards practical results, with no regard for the possible consequences. Thus, science is morally an imbecile, dishing up its confections blindly for whoever is able to use them. The likeliest user is always the exploiter —the manufacturer, military man, businessman and politician. Science produces what these highly motivated men require— processes characterised by repeatability and controllability, with which populations can be enchanted and enslaved.

For what, after all, is the politician's dream? It is a docile and predictable population, cheerful and well content with their compensations. This sheep-like state is precisely the great hope that the sciences hold out to us. For science is not deeply concerned about our differences but focuses instead on our similarities, the vulnerable places through which we can be manipulated and controlled.

If the unseen worlds that surround and interpenetrate us were ever understood according to the criteria of science, what a nightmare existence would become! For discovery is followed by exploitation, which is followed by laws which confirm the exploiters in the possession of their spoils. That is to say, after the scientist comes the industrialist, and after him comes the lawyer. And after the lawyer, cheerfully smiling, ready to explain the divine inevitability of it all, comes the cleric.

I did quite a lot of work organising these thoughts, in which I believe, but not to the point of obsession, and I thought of myself standing up here delivering them to you, and something seemed wrong. What was wrong was me trying to write the kind of speech that I thought you would expect a person like me to deliver to an audience like you.

Now that was a frightening thought, because it would mean that we had programmed each other in advance—you, knowing beforehand what to expect of me; and me, knowing what you would expect, shaping my product to meet that expectation.

What made matters even more difficult and complicated was knowing that my lecture was also going to appear in a book. That meant that it really had to be thoughtful and thought-provoking, detailed but concise, profound but easily understood —in a word, *heavy*. My words—these very words that I am now stammering forth—would have to stand up to the close scrutiny of the printed page, in company with the words of many truly fine thinkers who knew what they were talking about.

Now that is a really heavy pressure for a man like me who thinks of himself as a popular writer masquerading as a prophet and social commentator. For me it meant: Get deep! Use big words! Invent concepts! Dazzle them with footwork!

I guess it was then that I realised that I was a fantasist. My new topic would be "Science fiction: The Search for the Marvellous". Upon this I was going to base my career of substitute science fiction writer-speaker.

The fantasist is the representative of the people at large in the matter of non-ordinary reality. Himself unspecialised, a writer rather than a scientist or guru, he is the ombudsman of the general populace in the question of other worlds. Among other matters, the fantasy writer of popular tales concerns himself with who is to travel to the stars, who is to experience the magic of the unknown. It is a practical issue. It is the question, who is literally to experience the marvellous, the uncanny, the transcendental?

We fantasists most frequently make our heroes common men possessed of no special intellectual or spiritual attainments. Our intuition is that other-reality is not merely the province of a small élite, but the birthright of all humans.

I believe that many people read science fiction for a sense of participation in the wonders to come. The quest for non-ordinary reality is something more than curiosity and wishful thinking. We are too crowded in our everyday lives by replicas of ourselves and by the repetitious artifacts of our days and nights. But we do not quite believe in this prosaic world. Continually we are reminded of the strangeness of birth and death, the vastness of time and space, the unknowability of ourselves. One would like to live differently, more significantly. One would like to participate in events more meaningful than our daily round, feel sensations more exquisite than is our usual lot. One reads science fiction in order momentarily to transcend the dull quality of everyday life.

There is a reason behind this search for the ineffable. The death of God is argued by the theologians; but for most of us it is a fact of everyday life. 'God' is a word with unfortunate connotations for many. By it I mean the fundamental mystery forever untouched by our rationality. Even to call this mystery a mystery is to somehow limit it, somehow to fix it in our minds as a 'thing' of properties presently unknown but eventually to be learned precisely. This definition seems rational, but is in fact a contradiction of the very idea of the marvellous. The thing we lack is to be glimpsed but not captured. It is not to be defined, contained, or truly known.

This mystery is what we do not have any more. Our meagre substitute is the religion of man living on the Earth. We understand our ethical duties very well, we believe in them and try to follow them. But there is the secret sadness still remaining, the sense that we were born to quest, that our essence is unknowable, that we are plant and phantom, creatures of unknown dimensions. But all we come face to face with is our actual condition: we are ghosts smothered in bread and butter.

Science fiction, by its meretricious air, gives some of us hope. We have come to suspect anything that speaks of the Truth. We suspect that we are being lulled to sleep by these marvellous truths, always inapplicable to ourselves. An instinct tells us that the truth is to be stumbled upon in unlikely places. And what more unlikely place than in science fiction, which claims many things but does not claim to be literally true?

We wait for the coming of the unusual, the marvellous and strange, but it does not visit us. The postman comes, and the milkman, and the tax man, but not the herald of miraculous events. Take for example my own recent brush with the inexplicable.

I was driving home alone very late one night in Ibiza when I saw, to my left and low on the horizon, a large oval disk of yellow light. It seemed to be moving at high speed and it soon vanished.

At last, I thought, I have seen a flying saucer! In the spirit of scientific investigation, however, I stopped my car. The thing was gone. I backed the car, and the light appeared again, stationary this time against the blackness of a mountain.

After some minutes of study, I identified the object. It was light shining through a window of a house on the mountain. I studied it a while longer, and finally realised that it was coming from my own house. I had manufactured my own illusion, but then had not been clever enough to be taken in by it.

So where are we? We have broken out of the clockwork universes of Locke and Hume, and have discarded the materialistic view as hopelessly naïve. We have rejected the corresponding psychological view that we are no more than separate egoes each in his own sack of skin, living and dying alone. And although the ancient worlds of magic are lost to us, glimpses of new worlds are unfolding constantly.

This is the fantasist's world. The fantasist claims that no issue is irrevocably closed, no matter settled, no conclusion foregone. Fantasy, by its production of plausible but contradictory scenarios, by its acceptance of any premise, denies certainty and celebrates the vast horizons of the marvellous.

What is the marvellous? I think it is a glimpse of something that is in some fashion real, but unobtainable.

Where is the marvellous to be found? There are only two possible regions: the known, or the unknown, the here, or the there. Both have their advocates and explorers. The unknown is the obvious place to look—Oz, Atlantis, Ur, Far Centaurus. . . .

This is a logical outlook. Its main flaw is that so far it hasn't worked out. As we explore onwards, the regions of wonder retreat further away. Everywhere the explorer goes, he finds nothing more than creatures lawfully living their daily lives.

Many esoteric schools claim that the marvellous is to be located precisely *here*, in the commonplace, in our everyday life. In this view the difference between the marvellous and the commonplace is seen as a mental difference, a matter of perception on the observer's part rather than the discovery of something novel in the observed. In this view the marvellous is to be found by interior reconstruction; and this is to result in a rehabilitation of one's views of the external world.

This is a viewpoint of great force, and for many of us it makes immediate and intuitive sense. There are practical difficulties, however. Although the mystics have left us many ways and means for achieving this enlightened state of mind, few of us ever realise it. It is self-defeating to believe in a method when it does not bring the desired results, not for you nor for anyone you know.

The tool for encountering enlightenment is meditation—a word one usually intones in reverential manner. Meditation purports to do for the mind what organic foods do for the body. It is extremely good for you, although admittedly not as much fun as a good movie. Or even a bad movie.

It is a disarmingly simple practice, but there are difficulties. I have followed an ancient system of counting my breaths. You count up to ten, and then begin again, always focusing on the breath. Unfortunately, I usually lose count. And after I've lost count a few times I lose interest.

But when I finally do succeed in quieting my mind and achieving a measure of one-pointedness, something very strange happens. I find that I have plugged into my own internal music station. This music system broadcasts in my head continually, interrupted only by spot news flashes from 1951. I don't even like most of the stuff it dishes up, and the arrangements are uniformly terrible.

So, in my own experience, meditation is just like waiting at an airport, with its piped-in music and meaningless announcements. But with one important difference—in an airport you know that sooner or later you are going to take off and fly.

So much for meditation. And so much for backpacking through the inner world.

The machinery for probing inner experience is inaccessible. No one is going to tabulate and train our alpha rhythms, teach us techniques of trance, or explore our clairvoyant or telepathic powers.

The chemistry of inner experience is likewise proscribed. The governments forbid the ingestion of psychotropic drugs, perhaps in fear that we will all get, if not enlightened, at least high. Esotericism, which is legal, but not too much fun, prescribes to our condition. But when one tries to follow a spiritual path, nothing much happens for most of us. Faced with this lack of results, the esoteric schools put the blame squarely on us rather than on any insufficiency in their doctrines or methods. Finally, they explain our failure by taking refuge in paradoxes. They tell us, for example, that we can attain only by not wanting to attain —a neat double bind.

Some esoteric schools caution the disciple not to practise the extraordinary powers which we will acquire in the course of our work. This is surely an extraordinary statement. Most of us can't muster the power to give up smoking, much less to levitate.

As I went along writing my speech about the science fiction writer in his greater aspect of fantasist and explorer of the marvellous, I realised that never had the marvellous seemed so banal, irritating, and inadequate.

It should be apparent to you, as it finally was to me at that point, that I was taking myself very seriously. And this was funny since I had the reputation of being a humourist.

The truth of the situation burst upon me suddenly as I sat in my study trying to get my intonations right on the following line: 'These accounts of ancient wonders seem quaint and naïve to us now, as ours will someday seem to our descendants; but in their time they were attempts to get at the multifarious conditions of otherness, of creatures and circumstances unlike ourselves, the existence of which we believe in, but without the final sensory proof by which we might transform our lives.'

I can't even claim to know science fiction. I realise of course that I *write* it. But I don't try to write it. I don't sit down and say to myself, now I'm going to think up a science fiction idea. Let's see, shall it be unearthly monsters this time, or world-doom?

It really doesn't work that way. What happens is, something or other catches my attention, and a few words or images join together in a provocative manner. Or sometimes a whole scene leaps into my head.

Whatever it is, it simply comes. I don't tell it what it should be. It tells me. And what it usually turns out to be is another science fiction story.

As a matter of fact, I'm amazed at what has happened to science fiction in recent years. It has become a heavy academic field. And science fiction writers are being accorded a respect now, which I, as one of their peers and well-wishers, can only view with alarm and suspicion.

It seems like only yesterday, though it was in fact some 20 years ago, that all of us were writing pulp-action stories about a nebulous and ill-defined region that we called the future. Now our yarns are analysed in university classrooms for virtues we never suspected that they had. This is particularly true in America, the country that coined the word 'overkill' and then demonstrated its practical applications.

I, for one, have been caught unawares by this change in the evaluation of science fiction. Somehow, nobody told me that science fiction had gone respectable, that now I could be proud to declare that I was a science fiction writer. Back in the old days when people asked me what I did for a living, I said that I was a writer, and when they said what kind of a writer, and I told them, they said, 'Oh . . .'

It was not said hatefully. Just a little regretfully, as if for a moment they had thought they were meeting a real writer, and then discovered that you were actually a sort of word-carpenter. And you nodded with regret also, because in your heart of hearts you agreed with them.

You never met anyone who actually read science fiction in

those days: only people who had a friend who read science fiction. You never got the feeling that it was a really close friend, however.

And then, whammo—or so it seemed to me—suddenly science fiction was in, it was chic, it was flashy, it was meaningful, and it was a whole lot of fun. And it was also deep, very deep, it related to the issues of our times, and we science fiction writers with our shaky grammar and wind-up plots, our cardboard characters carrying a reluctant, half-born idea on their frail shoulders towards a formula conclusion—we, the *descamisados* of the fiction field—were heavy people and very much where it was at.

Being told that your writing has some relevance to something important is like being strapped into a strait jacket. Add to that the command 'be natural' and it's the same as being gagged. So naturally I set to work on this speech looking for the relevance that people said that science fiction writers had to some important issue.

There I was, sitting in my study getting ready to tell you some provocative stuff I had culled from the *Britannica* about Prester John. My cat was on the verge of having kittens. My razor had unaccountably vanished earlier that day, although I always put it back in the same place. There was no water in the cistern, and I had run out of cigarettes. All of this was going through my mind along with Atlantis and the nature of reality and other matters I was planning to enlighten you about.

It was all a senseless confusion. But then I thought, well, they really ought to know what to expect of me. If they read my work, which I seriously doubt, they know that I know little about science and less about the modern world. And my lack of awards ought to prove that I know nothing about science fiction.

And then it came to me: If these people had wanted a scholarly dissertation on some aspect of science fiction, they would have hired a scholarly dissertator. Not me.

This threw me into a considerable panic because my next thought was: In that case, what in God's name did they hire me to talk about?

At last I decided that they must have wanted me to talk about reality. For what else is there to talk about, finally, but reality?

198 · ROBERT SHECKLEY

What else is there to share opinions on? What else am I a student of, an expert on, what else am I forever exploring in the laboratory of my life?

Surely one of our foremost tasks is the testing and probing of ourselves and our interaction with the world. And in this, science and esotericism and all the systems of thought that man has evolved can be of no practical use. We are each of us alone in the vast regions within our skulls, testing the world with the make-shift instruments with which we were born.

In this talk I have tried to present some of my own reality, as far as I am able, at one particular time in my life. These are the things that make up my momentary universe. No summary is possible, even though I am at the end of my time here. Everything must remain unresolved, just as it in fact is. My subject matter escapes the neat confines of my definitions, for there is no datum that is not somehow pertinent to my situation. It is all part of the vast and uncompleted jigsaw puzzle that is our lives.

II

Man, Android and Machine

PHILIP K. DICK

PHILIP K. DICK

The saddest thing about the lecture series was the non-appearance of Philip K. Dick. He and Ursula Le Guin were the very first speakers that I invited to take part, and I had planned to frame the series around their two contributions, one at either end. Five years ago, the Philip K. Dick cult had not really got moving, but, at least in England today, it is more alive than I could have guessed. The advance bookings for the Dick lecture were the heaviest we received, and this delighted me more than I can say. Writers like Ursula Le Guin and Alan Garner can look after themselves. From almost the beginning, their books were taken up by prestigious publishers, and received ample attention from the serious critics. But for many years, Dick's fantastically involuted, inventive, elaborate series of novels, deeply involved in questions of perception, of appearance and reality—occupied with metaphysical questions far beyond the reach of the majority of his fellow writers' work—languished in the bargain basement, down in the pulp magazines and the genre publishers of cheap paperbacks. Only recently has he begun to receive the attention he has deserved for so long. (I've been telling people for eighteen years now, but I felt as if I were shouting into a vacuum that transmitted no sound.)

Anyway, he couldn't speak. His health is not good, and at the last moment it became clear that a trip to England from California would be far too great a strain. Disaster was averted by the extraordinary generosity of Robert Sheckley, who agreed to step in at the last minute, and won all hearts with the splendour of his performance. Disappointment has been averted for this book, too, because Phil kindly sent me the lecture he would have given, and here it is.

There are some truly lovely images in this article. As in Philip Dick's books, his imagery in the article below does not give up its essence immediately, or unambiguously. I am still uncertain, in some instances, whether he is speaking in metaphor, or giving what he believes to be the literal truth. My own inclination is to accept some of what he says as metaphoric, but really it doesn't matter.

I foresee the possibility that some readers will reject the

unorthodoxies of Dick's article as merely cranky, but I see something much more profound there than simple eccentricity. I would ask such readers to consider the coolness and sanity of Dick's fiction which, although it continually constructs worlds under pressure from the grossest of schizophrenias, catatonias and paranoias, maintains a serenity and humanity always in the narrative voice, which refuses to submit to the fragmenting and imperative forces of dissolution that the plot-lines evoke. He works in dangerous areas, and has amply demonstrated, many times over, a courage and a talent which have earned him the right to be listened to, and taken seriously. Sceptics, please suspend your disbelief.

Within the universe there exist fierce cold things, which I have given the name 'machines' to. Their behaviour frightens me, especially when it imitates human behaviour so well that I get the uncomfortable sense that these things are trying to pass themselves off as humans but are not. I call them 'androids', which is my own way of using that word. By 'android' I do not mean a sincere attempt to create in the laboratory a human being (as we saw in the excellent TV film *The Questor Tapes*). I mean a thing somehow generated to deceive us in a cruel way, to cause us to think it to be one of ourselves. Made in a laboratory—that aspect is not meaningful to me; the entire universe is one vast laboratory, and out of it come sly and cruel entities which smile as they reach out to shake hands. But their handshake is the grip of death, and their smile has the coldness of the grave.

These creatures are among us, although morphologically they do not differ from us; we must not posit a difference of essence, but a difference of behaviour. In my science fiction I write about them constantly. Sometimes they themselves do not know they are androids. Like Rachael Rosen, they can be pretty but somehow lack something; or, like Pris in *We Can Build You*, they can be absolutely born of a human womb and even design androids—the Abraham Lincoln one in that book—and themselves be without warmth; they then fall within the clinical entity 'schizoid', which means lacking proper feeling. I am sure we mean the same thing here, with the emphasis on the word 'thing'. A human being without the proper empathy or feeling is the same as an android built so as to lack it, either by design or mistake. We mean, basically, someone who does not care about the fate which his fellow living creatures fall victim to; he stands detached, a spectator, acting out by his indifference John Donne's theorem that 'No man is an island', but giving that theorem a twist: that which is a mental and moral island *is not a man.*

The greatest change growing across our world these days is probably the momentum of the living towards reification, and at the same time a reciprocal entry into animation by the mechanical. We hold now no pure categories of the living versus the non-living; this is going to be our paradigm: my character Hoppy, in *Doctor Bloodmoney,* who is a sort of human football within a maze of servo-assists. Part of that entity is organic, but all of it is alive; part came from a womb, all lives, and within the same universe. I am talking about our real world and not the world of fiction, when I say: one day we will have millions of hybrid entities which have a foot in both worlds at once. To define them as 'man' versus 'machine' will give us verbal puzzle-games to play with. What is and will be a real concern is: does the composite entity (of which Palmer Eldritch is a good example, among my characters), does he *behave* in a human way? Many of my stories contain purely mechanical systems which display kindness—taxicabs, for instance, or the little rolling carts at the end of *Now Wait For Last Year* which that poor defective human builds. 'Man' or 'human being' are terms which we must understand correctly and apply, but they apply not to origin or to any ontology but to a way of being in the world; if a mechanical construct halts in its customary operation to lend you assistance, then you will posit to it, gratefully, a humanity which no analysis of its transistors and relay-systems can elucidate. A scientist, tracing the wiring circuits of that machine to locate its humanness, would be like our own earnest scientists who tried in vain to locate the soul in man, and, not being able to find a specific organ located at a specific spot, opted to decline to admit that we have souls. As soul is to man, man is to machine: it is the added dimension, in terms of functional hierarchy. As one of us *acts* godlike (gives his cloak to a stranger), a machine *acts* human when it pauses in its programmed cycle to defer to it by reason of a decision.

But still, we must realise that the universe although kind to us in its entirety (it must like and accept us, or we would not be here; as Abraham Maslow says, 'otherwise nature would have executed us long ago') does contain grinning evil masks which loom out of the fog of confusion at us, and it may slay us for its own gain.

We must be careful, however, of confusing a mask, any mask, with the reality beneath. Think of the war-mask which Pericles placed over his features: you would behold a frozen visage, the grimness of war, without compassion—no genuine human face or person to whom you could appeal. And this was of course the intention. Suppose you did not even realise it was a mask; suppose you believed, as Pericles approached you in the fog and half-darkness of early morning, that this was his authentic countenance. Now, this is almost exactly how I described Palmer Eldritch in my novel about him: so much like the war-masks of the Attic Greeks that the resemblance cannot be accidental. Is, then, the hollow eyeslot, the mechanical metal arm and hand, the stainless-steel teeth, which are the dread stigmata of evil—is this not, this which I myself first saw in the overhead sky at noon one day back in 1963, a description, a vision, of a war-mask and metal armour, a god of battle? The God of Wrath who was angry with me. But under the anger, under the metal and helmet, there is, as with Pericles, the face of a man. A kind and loving man.

My theme for years in my writing has been, 'The devil has a metal face'. Perhaps this should be amended now. What I glimpsed and then wrote about was in fact not a face; it was a mask over a face. And the true face is the reverse of the mask. Of course it would be. You do not place fierce cold metal over fierce cold metal. You place it over soft flesh, as the harmless moth adorns itself artfully to terrorise others with ocelli. This is a defensive measure, and if it works, the predator returns to his lair grumbling, 'I saw the most frightening creature in the sky—wild grimaces and flappings, stingers and poisons.' His kin are impressed. The magic works.

I had supposed that only bad people wore frightening masks, but you can see now that I fell for the magic of the mask, its dreadful frightening magic, its *illusion*. I bought the deception and fled. I wish now to apologise for preaching that deception to you as something genuine: I've had you all sitting around the campfire with our eyes wide with alarm as I tell tales of the hideous monsters I encountered; my voyage of discovery ended in terrifying visions which I dutifully carried home with me as

I fled back to safety. Safety from what? From something which, when the need was gone for concealment, smiled and revealed its harmlessness.

Now I do not intend to abandon my dichotomy between what I call 'human' and what I call 'android', the latter being a cruel and cheap mockery of the former for base ends. But I had been going on surface appearances; to distinguish the categories more cunning is required. For if a gentle, harmless life conceals itself behind a frightening war-mask, then it is likely that behind gentle and loving masks there can conceal itself a vicious slayer of men's souls. In neither case can we go on surface appearance; we must penetrate to the heart of each, to the heart of the subject.

Probably everything in the universe serves a good end—I mean, serves the universe's goals. But intrinsic portions or sub-systems can be takers of life. We must deal with them as such, without reference to their rôle in the total structure.

The "Sepher Yezirah", a Cabbalist text, "The Book of Creation", which is almost 2,000 years old, tells us: 'God has also set the one over against the other; the good against the evil, and the evil against the good; the good proceeds from the good, and the evil from the evil; *the good purifies the bad, and the bad the good*; the good is preserved for the good, and the evil for the bad ones.'

Underlying the two game-players there is God, who is neither and both. The effect of the game is that both players become purified. Thus, the ancient Hebrew monotheism, so superior to our own view. We are creatures in a game with our affinities and aversions predetermined for us—not by blind chance but by patient, foresighted engramming systems which we dimly see. Were we to see them clearly, we would abolish the game. Evidently that would not serve anyone's interests. We must trust these tropisms, and anyhow we have no choice—not until the tropisms lift. And under certain circumstances they can and do. And at that point, much is clear which previously was occluded from us, intentionally.

What we must realise is that this deception, this obscuring of things as if under a veil—the veil of Maya, it has been called— this is not an end in itself, as if the universe is somehow perverse and likes to foil us *per se*; what we must accept, once we realise that a veil (called by the Greeks *dokos*) lies between us and reality, is that this veil serves a benign purpose. Parmenides, the pre-Socratic philosopher, is historically credited with being the first person in the West systematically to work out proof that the world cannot be as we see it, that *dokos*, the veil, exists. We see very much the same notion expressed by St Paul when he speaks about our seeing 'as if by the reflection on the bottom of a polished metal pan'. He is referring to the familiar notion of Plato's, that we see only images of reality, and probably these images are inaccurate and imperfect and not to be relied on. I wish to add that Paul was probably saying one thing more than Plato in the celebrated metaphor of the cave: Paul was saying that we may well be seeing the universe backwards.

The extraordinary thrust of this thought just simply cannot be taken in, even if we intellectually grasp it. 'To see the universe backwards?' What would that mean? Well, let me give you one possibility: that we experience time backwards; or more precisely, that our inner subjective category of experience of time (in the sense which Kant spoke of, a way by which we arrange experience), our time experience is orthogonal to the flow of time itself—at right angles. There are two times: the time which is our experience or perception or construct of ontological matrix, an extensiveness along with space as an inseparable extensiveness into another area—this is real, but the outer time-flow of the universe moves in a different direction. Both are real, but by experiencing time as we do, orthogonally to its actual direction, we get a totally wrong idea of the sequence of events, of causality, of what is past and what is future, where the universe is going.

I hope you realise the importance of this. Time is real, both as an experience in the Kantian sense, and real in the sense which the Soviet Dr Nikolai Kozyrev expresses it: that time is an energy, and it is the basic energy which binds the universe together, and upon which all life depends, all phenomena draw their source out of and express: it is the energy of each entelechy and of the total entelechy of the universe itself.

But time, in itself, is not moving from our past to our future. Its orthogonal axis leads it through a rotary cycle within which, for example, we have been 'spinning our wheels', so to speak, in a vast winter of our species that has lasted already about

2,000 of our lineal time years. Evidently orthogonal time or true time rotates something like the primitive cyclic time, within which each year was regarded as the same year, each new crop the same crop; in fact, each spring was the same spring again. What destroyed man's ability to perceive time in this overly simple way was that he himself as an individual spanned too many of these years and could see that he himself wore out, was not renewed each year like the corn crop, the bulbs and roots and trees. There had to be a more adequate idea of time than the simple cyclic time; so he developed, reluctantly, lineal time which is an accumulative time, as Bergson showed; it goes in only one direction and is added to—or adds to—everything as it sweeps along.

True orthogonal time is rotary, but on a vaster scale, much like the Great Year of the ancients; much, too, like Dante's idea of the time rate of eternity which you find expressed in his *Comedy*. During the Middle Ages such thinkers as Erigena had begun to sense true eternity or timelessness, but others had begun to sense that eternity involved time (timelessness would be a static state), although the time would be quite different from our perception of it. A clue lay in St Paul's reiteration that the Final Days of the world would be the Time of Restoration of All Things. He had evidently experienced this orthogonal time enough to understand that it contains in it as a simultaneous plane or extension everything which was, just as the grooves on an LP contain the part of the music which has already been played; they don't disappear after the stylus tracks them. A phonograph record is, actually, a long helical spiral, and can be represented entirely in a plane geometry sort of way: in space, although I suppose you can talk about the stylus accumulating the music as it goes along. The idea of dysfunctions such as bounce back and bounce forward are possible, here, but these would serve no teleological purpose: they would be time-slips, as in my novel *Martian Time-Slip*. Yet, if they were to occur, they would serve a purpose for us, the observer or listener: we would suddenly learn a great deal more about our universe. I believe these ontological dysfunctions in time do occur, but that our brains automatically generate false memory-systems to obscure them, at once. The reason for this carries back to my premise: the veil or *dokos* is there to deceive

us for a good reason, and such disclosures as these time dysfunctions make are to be obliterated that this benign purpose
be maintained.

Within a system which must generate an enormous amount
of veiling, it would be vainglorious to expostulate on what
actuality is, when my premise declares that were we to penetrate to it for any reason this strange veil-like dream would
reinstate itself retroactively, in terms of our perceptions and in
terms of our memories. The mutually dreaming would resume
as before, because, I think, we are like the characters in my
novel *Ubik*; we are in a state of half-life. We are neither dead
nor alive, but preserved in cold storage, waiting to be thawed
out. Expressed in the perhaps startlingly familiar terms of the
procession of the seasons, this is winter of which I speak; it is
winter for our race, and it is winter in *Ubik* for those in half-life.
Ice and snow cover them; ice and snow cover our world in
layers of accretions, which we call *dokos* or Maya. What melts
away the rind or layer of frozen ice over the world each year is
of course the reappearance of the sun. What melts the ice and
snow covering the characters in *Ubik*, and which halts the
cooling-off of their lives, the entropy which they feel, is the
voice of Mr Runciter, their former employer, calling to them.
The voice of Mr Runciter is none other than that same voice
which each bulb and seed and root in the ground, our ground,
in our wintertime, hears. It hears: 'Wake up! Sleepers awake!'
Now I have told you who Runciter is, and I have told you our
condition and what *Ubik* is really about. What I have said, too,
is that time is actually as Dr Kozyrev in the Soviet Union
supposes it to be, and in *Ubik* time has been nullified and no
longer moves forward in the lineal fashion which we experience.
As this has happened, due to the deaths of the characters, we
the readers and they the personae see the world as it is without
the veil of Maya, without the obscuring mists of lineal time. It
is that very energy, Time, postulated by Dr Kozyrev as binding
together all phenomena and maintaining all life, which by its
activity hides the ontological reality beneath its flow.

The orthogonal time axis may have been represented in my
novel *Ubik* without my understanding what I was depicting:
i.e. the form-regression of objects along an entirely different
line from that out of which they, in lineal time, were built. This

reversion is that of the Platonic Ideas or archetypes: a rocket-ship reverts to a Boeing 747, then back to a World War I 'Jenny' biplane. While I may indeed have expressed a dramatic view of orthogonal time, it is less certain that this is orthogonal time *undergoing an unnatural reversion*: i.e. moving backwards. What the characters in *Ubik* see may be orthogonal time moving along its normal axis; if we ourselves somehow see the universe reversed, then the 'reversions' of form which objects in *Ubik* undergo may be momentum towards perfection. This would imply that our world as extensive in time (rather than extensive in space) is like an onion, an almost infinite number of successive layers. If lineal time seems to add layers, then perhaps orthogonal time peels these off, exposing layers of progressively greater Being. One is reminded here of Plotinus's view of the universe as consisting of concentric rings of emanation, each one possessing more Being—or reality—than the next.

Within that ontology, that realm of Being, the characters, like ourselves, slumber in dreams as they wait for the voice which will awaken them. When I say that they and we are waiting for spring to come I am not merely using a metaphor. Spring means thermal return, the abolition of the process of entropy; their life can be expressed in terms of thermal units, and those units have left. It is spring which restores that life—restores it fully and in some cases, as with our species, the new life is a metamorphosis; the period of slumbering is a period of gestation together with our fellows which will culminate in an entirely different form of life than we have ever known before. Many species are this way; they go through cycles. Thus, our winter sleep is not a mere 'spinning of our wheels' as it might seem. We will not simply bloom again and again with the same blossoms we produced each year before. This is why it was an error for the ancients to believe that for us, as for the vegetable world, the same year returned; for us, there is accumulation, the growth of an entelechy for each of us not yet perfected or completed, and never repeatable. Like a symphony of Beethoven, each of us is unique, and, when this long winter is over, we as new blooms will surprise ourselves and the world around us. What we will do, many of us, is throw off the mere masks which we have worn—masks which were intended to be taken for reality. Masks which have successfully fooled everyone, as is their purpose. We have been so many Palmer Eldritches moving through the cold fog and mists and twilight of winter, but now soon we will emerge and lift the war-mask of iron to reveal the face within.

It is a face which we, the wearers of the masks, have not seen either; it will surprise us, too.

For absolute reality to reveal itself, our categories of space-time experiences, our basic matrix through which we encounter the universe, must break down and then utterly collapse. I dealt with this breakdown in *Martian Time-Slip* in terms of time; in *Maze of Death* there are endless parallel realities arranged spacially; in *Flow My Tears, The Policeman Said* the world of one character invades the world in general and shows that by 'world' we mean nothing more or less than Mind—the immanent Mind which thinks—or rather dreams—our world. That dreamer, like the dreamer in Joyce's *Finnegans Wake*, is stirring and about to come to consciousness. We are within that dream; these manifold dreams are about to fold into themselves, to disappear as dreams, to be replaced by the true landscape of the dreamer's reality. We will join him as he sees it once again and is aware that he has been dreaming. In Brahmanism, we would say that a great cycle has ended and that Brahman stirs and wakes again, or that it falls asleep from being awake; in any case the universe which we experience which is an extension in space and time of its Mind is experiencing the typical dysfunctions that take place at the end of a cycle. You may say if you prefer, 'Reality is collapsing; it's all turning to chaos', or, with me, you may wish to say, 'I feel the dream, the *dokos*, lifting; I feel Maya dissolving: I am waking up, He is waking up: I am the Dreamer: we are all the Dreamer'. One thinks here of Arthur Clarke's Overmind.

Each of us is going to have either to affirm or deny the reality which is revealed when our ontological categories collapse. If you feel that chaos is closing in, that when the dream fades out, nothing will be left, or, worse, something dreadful will confront you—well, this is why the concept of the Day of Wrath persists; many people have a deep intuition that when the *dokos* abruptly melts they're in for a hard time of it. Perhaps so. But I think that the visage revealed will be a smiling one, since spring usually beams down on creatures rather than blasting them with desiccating heat. There may, too, be malign forces in the universe which will be revealed by the removal of the veil, but I think about the fall of the political tyranny in the US in 1974 and it seems to me that the exposure to the light of day of that ugly cancer and its subsequent removal is the nature of high value in disclosure to sunlight; we may have to suffer such shocks as learning that during the *Nacht und Nebel*, during the time of night and fog, our freedom, our rights, our property and even our lives were mutilated, deformed, stolen and destroyed by base creatures glutting themselves in spurious sanctuary down there at San Clemente and in Florida and all the other villas, but the shock of exposure was worse for their plans than it was for ours. Our plans called only for us to live with justice and truth and freedom; the former government of this country had arranged to live with cruel power of the most arrogant sort, while at the same time lying to us ceaselessly through all the channels of communication. Such is a good example of the healing power of sunlight; this power first to reveal and then to shrivel up the coarse plant of tyranny which had grown deep into the beating heart of a good people.

That heart beats on now, more strongly than ever, although it was admittedly badly engulfed; but the cancer which had crawled through it—that cancer is gone. That black growth which shunned light, shunned truth, and destroyed anyone who told the truth—it shows what can flourish during the long winter of the human race. But that winter began to end in the vernal equinox of 1974.

Sometimes I think that the Dreamer began to press against the tyranny as he, the Dreamer, woke us; here in the United States he woke us to our condition, our awful peril.

One of the best novels, and most important to an understanding of the nature of our world, is Ursula Le Guin's *The Lathe of Heaven*, in which the dream universe is articulated in such a striking and compelling way that I hesitate to add any further explanation to it; it requires none. I do not think that either of us had read about Charles Tart's study of dreams when we wrote our several novels, but I have now, and I have read some of Robert E. Ornstein, he being the 'brain revolution' person north of where I live, at Stanford University. From Ornstein's work it would appear that there is a possibility that we have two entirely separate brains, rather than one brain divided into two bilaterally equal hemispheres, that, in fact, whereas we have a body we have two minds (I refer to you the article by Joseph E. Bogen, "The Other Side of the Brain: An Appositional Mind", published in Ornstein's collection *The Nature Of Human Consciousness*). Bogen demonstrates that every now and then a researcher began to scent the possibility that we have two brains, two minds, but that only with modern brain-mapping techniques and related studies has it been possible to demonstrate this. For example, in 1763 Jerome Gaub wrote: '. . . I hope that you will believe Pythagoras and Plato, the wisest of the ancient philosophers, who, according to Cicero, divided the mind into two parts, one partaking of reason and the other devoid of it.' Bogen's article contains concepts so fascinating as to cause me to wonder why we never realised that our so-called 'unconscious' is not an unconscious at all but another consciousness, with which we have a tenuous relationship. It is this other mind or consciousness which dreams us at night—we are its audience as it binds us in its story telling; we are little children spellbound . . . which is why *Lathe Of Heaven* may represent one of the basic great books of our civilisation, especially since Ursula Le Guin, I'm sure, arrived at her formulation without knowledge of Ornstein's work and Bogen's extraordinary theory. What is involved here is that one brain receives exactly the same input as the other, through the various sense channels, but processes the information differently; each brain works in its own unique way (the left is like a digital computer; the right much like an analogue computer, working by comparing patterns). Processing the identical information each may arrive at a totally different result—whereupon, since our personality is constructed in our left brain, if the right brain finds something vital which we to its left remain unaware of, it must communicate during sleep, during the dream; hence, the Dreamer who communicates to us so urgently in the night is located neurologically, evidently, in our right brain, which is the not-I. But more than that (for instance, is the right brain as Bergson thought perhaps a transducer or transformer for ultra-sensory informational input beyond the purview of the left?) we can't say as yet. I think, though, that the spell of *dokos* is woven by our right brain's plural; we as a species are prone to reside entirely within one hemisphere only, leaving the other to do what it must to protect us, and to protect the world. Keep in mind that this protectiveness is bilateral, an exchange between the world and each of us: each of us is a treasure, to be cherished and preserved, but so is the world and the hidden seeds in it, slumbering. The other hidden seeds. Thus, through the veil-spinning of Kali, the right hemisphere of each of us, we are kept ignorant of what we must be ignorant of now. But that time is ending; that winter is melting, along with its terrors, its tyrannies and snow.

The best description of this *dokos*-veil formation that I've read yet appears in an article in *Science-Fiction Studies*, March 1975, by Frederic Jameson, in "After Armageddon: Character Systems in *Dr Bloodmoney*", which is an obscure novel of mine. I quote '. . . Every reader of Dick is familiar with this nightmarish uncertainty, this reality fluctuation, sometimes accounted for by drugs,* sometimes by schizophrenia,* and sometimes by new SF powers, in which the psychic world as it were goes outside, and reappears in the form of simulacra or of some photographically cunning reproduction of the external.' (p. 32) (*I hope Jameson means drugs in the writing and schizophrenia in the writing, not in me, but I'll let that pass.)

You can see from Jameson's description that we are talking about something very like Maya here, but also something very like a hologram. I have the distinct feeling that Carl Jung was correct about our unconsciousnesses, that they form a single entity or as he called it 'collective unconscious'. In that case, this collective brain entity, consisting of literally billions of 'stations', which transmit and receive, would form a vast network of communication and information, much like Teilhard's concept of the noösphere. This *is* the noösphere, as real as the ionosphere or the biosphere; it is a layer in our earth's atmosphere composed of holographic and informational projections in a unified and continually processed Gestalt the sources of which are our manifold right brains. This constitutes a vast Mind, immanent within us, of such power and wisdom as to seem, to us, equal to the Creator. This was Bergson's view of God anyhow.

It is interesting how deeply troubled the brilliant Greek philosophers were by activities of the gods; they could see the activities and (or so they thought) the gods themselves, but as Xenophanes put it: 'Even if a man should chance to speak the most complete truth, yet he himself does not know it; all things are wrapped in *appearances*.'

This notion came to the pre-Socratics by virtue of their seeing the many but knowing *a priori* that what they saw could not be real, since only the One existed.

'If God is all things, then appearances are certainly deceptive; and, though observation of the kosmos may yield generalisations and speculations about God's plans, true knowledge of them could only be had by a direct contact with God's mind.' (I am quoting Edward Hussey in his marvellous book *The Pre-Socratics*, p. 35.) And he goes on to give two fragments of Heraclitus: 'The nature of things is in the habit of concealing itself.' (Fragment 123) 'Latent structure is master of obvious structure.' (Fragment 54)

I wish to remind you that the ancient Greeks and Hebrews did not conceive of God or God's Mind as above the universe, but within it: immanent Mind or immanent God, with the visible universe the body of God, so that God was to universe as psyche is to soma. But they also conjectured that perhaps God was not the great psyche but noös, a different sort of mind; in which case, the universe was not his body but God Himself. The space-time universe houses but is not a part of God; what is God is the vast grid-field or energy field alone.

If you assume (and you'd be correct to do so) that our minds are energy fields of some kind anyhow, and that we are fundamentally interacting fields, rather than discrete particles, then there is no theoretical problem in grasping this interaction between the billions of brain-prints emanating and forming and reforming into the patterns of the noösphere. However, if you still hold to the nineteenth-century view of yourself as a brittle organism, much like a machine, made up of parts—well, you see, then how can you merge with the noösphere? You are a unique concrete thing. And thing-ness is what we must get away from, in regarding ourselves and in considering life. By more modern views we are overlapping fields, all of us, animals included, plants included. This is the ecosphere and we are all in it. But what we don't realise is that the billions of discrete and entirely ego-oriented left-hemisphere brains have far less to say about the ultimate disposition of this world than does the collective noöspheric Mind which comprises all our right brains, and in which each of us shares. *It* will decide, and I do not think it impossible that this vast plasmic noösphere, considering that it covers our entire planet in a veil or layer, may interact outwards into solar-energy fields and from there into cosmic fields. Each of us, then, partakes of the cosmos—if he is willing to listen to his dreams. And it is his dreams which will transform him from a mere machine into an authentic human. He will no longer strut about and clank with majestic iron, no longer rule his little kingdom here; he will soar upwards, flying like a field of negative ions, like the entity Ubik in my novel of that name: being life and giving life, but never defining himself because no clearcut name to him—to us—can be given.

As we move up the manifold—i.e. progress forwards in lineal time, or somehow stand still and lineal time progresses forwards, whichever model is more correct—we as many entelechies are continually signalled, given information, and most of all, disinhibited by firings from the universe around us; in this fashion harmony among all parts of the universe is maintained. There is no more grand scheme than this: to be aware that I, as a representative entelechy, must unfold only as these preset signals reach me, and that control as to the when—the locus in time—that each signal will come is entirely in the hands of the universe . . . this is a thrilling comprehension, and makes me aware of the unbreakable tie between me and my environment.

There is such order in the response between engrammed systems within each of us and the accumulating signals which fire these systems in sequence as to imply that the Agency which laid down the entelechy in the first place, engrammed and then blocked these systems, knew with absolute precision where along the time path the signals would take place which would disinhibit; chance is not involved—the happiest of accidents is the most astute planning of the universe.

Sometimes I wonder how we could have imagined that our species was exempt from the instincts which lower species obviously have. What is different about us, however, is that all ants, for instance, are disinhibited by the same signal, and the same behaviour occurs; it is as if one ant again and again is involved, endlessly. But for us, each is a unique entelechy, and each receives unique sequences of signals—to which each responds uniquely. Still, this is the language of the universe which the ant hears; we thrill with a common joy.

I myself have derived much of the material for my writing from dreams. In *Flow My Tears*, for example, the powerful dream which comes to Felix Buckman near the end, the dream of the wise old man on horseback, that was an actual dream I had at the time of writing the novel. In *Martian Time-Slip* I've written in so many dream experiences that I can't separate them, now, when I read the novel.

Ubik was primarily a dream, or series of dreams. In my opinion it contains strong themes of pre-Socratic philosophical views of the world, unfamiliar to me when I wrote it (to name just one, the views of Empedocles). It is possible that the noösphere contained thought patterns in the form of very weak energy until we developed radio transmission; whereupon the energy level of the noösphere went out of bounds and assumed a life of its own. It no longer served as a mere passive repository of human information (the "Seas of Knowledge" which ancient Sumer believed in) but, due to the incredible surge of charge from our electronic signals and the information-rich material therein, we have given it power to cross a vast threshold; we have, so to speak, resurrected what Philo and other ancients called the *Logos*. Information has, then, become alive, with a collective mind of its own independent of our brains, if this theory is correct. It does not merely know what we know and remember what once was known, but can construct solutions on its own: it is a titanic AI system. The difference would be between a tape recorder which could 'remember' a Beethoven symphony which it 'heard', and one which could create new ones, on and on; the library in the sky, having read all the books there are and ever were, is writing its own book, now, and at night we are being read to—told the exciting tale comprising that Great Work-in-Progress.

I must mention Ian Watson's article in *Science-Fiction Studies* on Le Guin's *Lathe Of Heaven*; in his excellent piece he refers to what may be the most significant—startlingly so—story SF has yet produced: Fredric Brown's story that appeared in *Astounding*, "The Waveries". You must read that story; if you do not you may die without understanding the universe coming into being around you. The Waveries were attracted to Earth by our radio waves; they returned in facsimile form, so like our transmissions (SOS and so forth, chronologically) that at first we couldn't fathom what was up. Regarding *Lathe*, Watson says:

> ... Conceivably George [Orr] dreamt a hostile invasion into a peaceful one; yet the dominant probability is that the aliens are, as they maintain, 'of the dream time', that their whole culture revolves around the mode of 'reality dreaming itself into being', that they have been attracted to Earth like the Waveries of Fredric Brown's story, only by dream-waves rather than radio waves. (pp. 71–2)

This could be considered scary stuff, this theme in Le Guin's work and mine. What are dreams? Are there these dream-universe entities that have come here from another star (Aldebaran, in Ms Le Guin's novel)? Are the UFOs that people see holograms projected by their unconscious minds, acting as transformers, acting, too, as transducers of these strange dream-universe creatures?

For the past year I've had many dreams which seemed—I stress the world 'seemed'—to indicate that a telepathic communication was in progress somewhere within my head, but after talking with Henry Korman, an associate of Ornstein's, I would imagine that it is merely my right and left hemispheres conferring in a Martin Büber I-and-Thou dialogue. But much of the dream material seemed beyond my personal ability to have created. At one point an attempt was made to get me to write down a complex engineering principle which was shown me in the form of a round motor with twin rotating wheels, opposed in direction, much as Yin and Yang in Taoism alternate as opposing pairs (and much like Empedocles saw love versus strife, the dialectic interaction of the world). But this was a true engineering device they had there in my dream; they showed me a pencil, they said, 'This principle was known in *your* time.' And as I rushed to find a pencil they added: 'Known, but buried in a basement and forgotten.' There was an elaborate high torque chain-thrown mechanism which moved cam-wise between the two rotors, but I never got the hang of it, when I woke up. What I did later on grasp, though, was this: further dreams made it clear that somehow our treatment of seawater by an osmosis process would give us not only pure water but a source of energy as well. However, they had the wrong human when they began giving me that sort of material; I am not trained to understand it. I did purchase over a thousand dollars worth of reference books to try to figure out what I'd been shown, though. I have learned this: something to do with a high hysteresis factor, in this twin-rotor system, is converted from a defect to an advantage. No braking mechanism is needed; the two rotors spin constantly at the same velocity, and torque is transferred by a thrown cam-chain.

I give this illustration only to show that either my unconscious has been reading articles on engineering which elude my memory and my conscious attention and interest, or there are, shall I say, dream-universe people from, shall I say, Aldebaran or some other star with us. Perhaps joining their noösphere with ours? And offering assistance to a crippled, blighted planet which has been bogged down, like a rat on a weary wheel, in the dead of winter for over 2,000 years? If they bring the springtime with them, then whoever they are, I welcome them; like Joe Chip in *Ubik*, I fear the cold, the weariness; I fear the death of wearing out on endless upwards stairs, while someone cruel, or anyhow wearing a cruel mask, watches and offers no aid—the machine, lacking empathy, watching as mere spectator, the same horror which I know haunts Harlan Ellison. It is perhaps more frightening than the killer himself (in *Ubik* it was Jory), this figure which sees but gives no assistance, offers no hand. That is the android, to me, and the evil demigod to Harlan; we both shudder at the idea of its existence. What I can tell you about the dream-universe people, is that if they do exist, whoever they are, they are not that unsympathetic android; they are human in this deepest of all senses: they have reached out a helping hand to our planet, to our polluted ecosphere, and perhaps even assisted in throwing down the tyranny which gripped the United States, Portugal, Greece, and one day they will throw down the tyranny of the Soviet bloc as well. This is what I think of when I grasp the idea of springtime: the lifting of the iron doors of the prison and the poor prisoners, in Beethoven's *Fidelio*, let out into the sunlight. Ah, that moment in the opera, when they see the sun and feel its warmth. And at last, at the end, the trumpet call of freedom sounds the permanent end of their cruel imprisonment; help, *from outside*, has arrived.

Every now and then someone comes up to a science fiction writer, smiles a crazy secret in-the-know smile and smirks, 'I know that what you're writing is true, and it's in code. All you SF writers are receivers for Them.' Naturally I ask who 'Them' is. The answer is always the same. 'You know. Up there. The space people. They're already here, and they're using your writing. You know it, too.'

I kind of smile and edge off. It keeps happening. Well, I hate to admit it, but it is possible that there is (one) such a thing as telepathy; and (two) that the CETI project's idea that we might communicate with extra terrestrial beings via telepathy is possibly a reasonable idea—if telepathy exists and if ETIs exist. Otherwise we are trying to communicate with someone who doesn't exist with a system which doesn't work. At least that'll keep a lot of us busy for a long, long time. But I understand now that a Soviet astronomy bunch, evidently headed by the same Dr Nikolai Kozyrev who developed the time-as-energy theory I mentioned previously, has reported receiving signals from an ETI *within* our solar system. If this were true, and our people are saying that the Soviets are just monitoring stale, flat and unprofitable old signals from our own discarded satellites and other junk ships—well, suppose these ETI entities or corporate mind are within, say, the great plasma which seems to surround Earth and is involved with solar flares and the like; I refer of course to the noösphere. It is ETI and TI at once, and possibly bears a strong resemblance to what Ms Le Guin has written about in *Lathe*. And as every SF fan knows, my own works deal with similar themes ... thus giving an annoying couple of marks for plausibility to these freaks who are forever lurching up to every SF author and saying, 'What you're writing is in code ...,' etc. In truth, we may be influenced, especially during dream states, by a noösphere which is a product of our own, capable of independent mentation, and involved with ETIs, a mixture of all three and God knows what else. This might not be the Creator, but it would be as close to Infinite Mind as we might get, and close enough. That it is benign is obvious, to recall Maslow's remarks that if nature didn't like us it would have executed us long ago—here read Infinite Noösphere for nature.

We humans, the warm-faced and tender, with thoughtful eyes—we are perhaps the true machines. And those objective constructs, the natural objects around us and especially the electronic hardware we build, the transmitters and microwave relay stations, the satellites, they may be cloaks for authentic living reality inasmuch as they may participate more fully and in a way obscured to us in the ultimate Mind. Perhaps we see not only a deforming veil, but backwards. Perhaps the closest approximation to truth would be to say: 'Everything is equally alive, equally free, equally sentient, because everything is not alive or half-alive or dead, but rather *lived through*.' Radio signals are boosted by a transmitter; they pass *through* the various components, modified and augmented, their contours changed, noise eliminated and rejected . . . we are extensions, like those metal arms which pick up radioactive objects for scientists. We are gloves which God puts on in order to move things here and there as He wishes. For some reason He prefers to handle reality this way (I will not budge but will defend that pun).

We are suits of clothing which He creates, puts on and uses and finally discards. We are suits of armour, too. Which gives a misleading impression to certain other butterflies within certain other suits of armour. Within the armour is the butterfly and within the butterfly is—the signal from another star. In the novel I am writing (which the Dreamer, perhaps, is expressing through me) that star is called Albemuth. I hadn't read Ms Le Guin's novel *Lathe Of Heaven* when the idea came to me, but the reader of that novel will find there also what I just now meant by our being stations within a vast grid—and not realising it.

Consider this Meditation of Rumi, a Sufi saying by Idries Shah, who is a favourite among modern Sufis: 'The worker is hidden in the workshop'.

Since it is evident that more than anyone else Dr Ornstein has pioneered the way to discover the new worldview, which involves a bilateral brain parity unsuspected since the time of Pythagoras and Plato, I recently summoned my courage and wrote him. Fans now and then write me, their hands shaking

nervously; my entire typewriter shook nervously as I wrote to
Dr Ornstein. Here is the text of my letter, which I place here as
a final note to explain how I have transcended the categories of
reality-versus-illusion by his help, and thus brought into clear
sight an end to 20 years' study and effort on my part. I quote:

Dear Dr Ornstein:
 Recently I met Mr Henry Korman and Mr Tony Hiss (Tony
had come to interview me for the *New Yorker*). I got into a
marvellous discussion with Henry about Sufism and I mentioned my admiration, bordering on fanatic enthusiasm, for
your pioneer work with bilateral brain hemispheric parity.
Thus, I, having learned that they know you, am summoning my
courage to write you and ask, What has become of me, since
experimenting with bringing on my right hemisphere (I did it
mainly by the ortho molecular formula vitamins, plus a good
deal of concentrated meditation)?
 By this I mean to say, Dr Ornstein, ten months ago this took
place, and for ten months I have been a different person. But
what to me is most extraordinary (I am writing a book about it,
but in the form of fiction, a novel called *To Scare The Dead*) is
that—well, let me give the premise as I placed it into the novel:
 Nicholas Brady, an ordinary American citizen with contemporary worldly values and drives (money and power and
prestige) suddenly has inside him a winking into life of an entity
which has slumbered for 2,000 years. This entity is an Essene,
who died knowing that he would be given the promised resur-
rection; he knew it because he and other Qumran individuals
had in their possession secret formulae and medications and
scientific practices to insure it. So suddenly our protagonist,
Nicholas Brady, finds that there are two of him: his old self, at
his secular job and goals, and this Essene from the Qumran
wadi back circa 45 A.D., a holy man with holy values and utter
antagonism to the secular physical world, which he sees as the
'City of Iron'. The Qumran mind takes over and directs Brady
in a complicated series of acts until it becomes evident that
others such as this Qumran man are coming back to life here
and there in the world.
 Studying the Bible, along with this Qumran personality,

Brady finds that the *New Testament* is in cipher. The Qumran personality can read it. 'Jesus' is really Zagreus-Zeus, taking two forms, one mild, the other utterly powerful, on which his followers can draw when in need.

The Qumran personality, who, for fictional purposes, I call Thomas, gradually informs Brady that these are the Parousia, the Final Days. And to be prepared; Thomas will prepare him by reminding him of his own divinity—anamnesis, Thomas calls it. Thomas develops a special parity relationship with Brady, but evolves as a source of teaching for the incredibly ignorant Brady the entity known as Erasmus, who is in fact a station in the noösphere, which is now so fully charged around Earth that if you are aware of it you can consciously, rather than unconsciously, draw from it; these are the 'Seas of Knowledge' which were known in ancient times and upon which the Sibyl at Delphi drew. But this is a cover, because Brady realises that in point of fact, the Qumran men had as their god not the mythical Jesus but the actual Zagreus, and by doing research, Brady soon learns that Zagreus was a form of Dionysos. Christianity is a later form of the worship of Dionysos, refined through the strange and lovely figure of Orpheus. Orpheus, like Jesus, is real only in the sense that Dionysos is becoming socialised; born here as a child of another race, not a human one but a visiting race, Zagreus has had to learn by degrees to modify his 'madness', which is now kept to a low ebb. Basically, he is with us to reconstruct us as expressions of him, and the MO of this is our being possessed by him—which the early Christians sought for, and hid from the hated Romans. Dionysos-Zagreus-Orpheus-Jesus was always pitted against the City of Iron, be it Rome or Washington, DC; he is the god of springtime, of new life, of small and helpless creatures, he is the god of mirth and frenzy, and of sitting here day after day working on this novel.

But in the novel, Thomas says, 'The Final Days have come. The overthrow of the tyranny is that which, in lurid language, John described in *Revelation*. Jesus-Zagreus is seizing his own, now, one after another; *he lives again.*'

During winter, it was believed that Dionysos, the god of the vine plant, of vegetation, of the crop, slumbered. It was known that no matter how dead he seemed (James Joyce's

Finnegans Wake is a wonderful account of this, where they accidentally spill beer on the corpse and it revives) he was actually alive, though you'd never know it. And then—not to the surprise of those who understood him and believed in him—he was reborn. His followers knew he would be; they knew the secret ('Behold! I tell you a sacred secret', etc.). We are speaking here of the mystery religions, all of them, including Christianity. Our God has been sleeping, during the long winter of the human culture (not for one year's rotational cycle of seasons, but from 45 A.D. through the centuries of mental winter to now); just when winter holds all in its grip, the snow of despair and defeat (in our case, political chaos, moral ruin, economic ruin— the winter of our planet, our world, our civilisation) then the vine, which was gnarled and old and seemingly dead, breaks into new life, and our God is reborn—not outside us as such, but in each of us. Slumbering not under snow over the ground-surface but within the right hemispheres of our brains. We have been waiting, we didn't know for what. This is it: this is spring for our planet, in a deeper more fundamental way. The cold chains of iron are being thrown off, but by what a miracle. As with my character, Nicholas Brady—I've had Zagreus awaken in my right hemisphere, and felt the flooding of renewed life, his vigour, his personality, and his godlike wisdom; he hated the injustice he saw around him, and the lies, and he remembered 'The dear lone lands untroubled by men, where amid the shadowy green/The little ones of the forest live unseen' (Euripides). Dr Ornstein, thank you for helping bring winter to an end, and ushering in—not just spring—but the living life of Spring alive but asleep inside us.

Really, I suppose that the clear line between hallucination and reality has itself become a kind of hallucination, and perhaps I am taking my dream experiences too seriously. But there is much interest now, for instance, in the Senoi tribe of the Malay Peninsula (*vide* Kilton Stewart's article "Dream Theory in Malaya" in Charles T. Tart's *Altered States of Consciousness*). In a dream I was shown that the word 'Jesus' is a code, a neologism and not a real name at all; those reading the text in those early days who were the esoteri (the Qumran men,

possibly) would see 'Zeus' and 'Zagreus' combined into the integer 'Jesus'. It is a substitution code, I think they call it. Now, ordinarily, one would not give much credit to such a dream, or rather to any dream insofar as it might be an actual entity, an AI system for instance, giving you accurate information which you otherwise would not have available to you. But as I went to one of my textbooks the other day to check a spelling, I found these remarkably similar textual passages, the first of which we all know, since it concludes our own sacred writings, the *New Testament*: '. . . I am the root and scion of David, the bright morning star.' (*Revelation* 22:16, Jesus describing himself.)
And:

> Of all the trees that are
> He hath his flock, and feedeth root by root,
> The Joy-god Dionysos, the pure star
> That shines amid the gathering of the fruit.

(Pindar, a favourite quatrain of Plutarch, circa 430 B.C.).

What are names? This is the god of in-toxication, taking in the sacred mushroom (cf. John Allegro) or wine, or finding a joke so terribly funny that you lose all reason laughing and crying, as when you see one of the slapstick silent comedies. In the one short stanza of Pindar we have flock, we have trees, we have in addition to these two major symbols of Jesus, terms by which all the esoteri recognise him yet, two more inner terms: the root and star.

The reference to 'root and star' might be taken as equal to a spacial extension of the time extension of 'I am Alpha and Omega', which is, the first and last. So 'root and star' indicate: I am from the chthonic world up, and the starry heaven downwards. But I see something else in star, in bright morning star: I think he was saying, 'The signal that the springtime for man is here, that signal comes from another star.' We have friends and they are ETI, and it is, as He told us, a bright and morning star: the star of love.